Let Dem Know

The iconic poetry of

BENJAMIN ZEPHANIAH

Let Dem Know

PUFFIN

PUFFIN BOOKS

UK | USA | Canada | Ireland | Australia
India | New Zealand | South Africa

Puffin Books is part of the Penguin Random House group of companies
whose addresses can be found at global.penguinrandomhouse.com

www.penguin.co.uk
www.puffin.co.uk
www.ladybird.co.uk

Penguin Random House UK

The poems in this collection were originally published in *Talking Turkeys* (1994), *Funky Chickens* (1996) and *Wicked World* (2000)

This collection first published 2026
001

Printed in Great Britain by Clays Ltd, Elcograf S.p.A.

The authorized representative in the EEA is Penguin Random House Ireland, Morrison Chambers, 32 Nassau Street, Dublin D02 YH68

A CIP catalogue record for this book is available from the British Library

ISBN: 978–0–241–78970–4

All correspondence to:
Puffin Books
Penguin Random House Children's
One Embassy Gardens, 8 Viaduct Gardens, London SW11 7BW

FSC www.fsc.org MIX Paper FSC® C018179

Penguin Random House is committed to a sustainable future for our business, our readers and our planet. This book is made from Forest Stewardship Council® certified paper.

CONTENTS

Poems from the Last Person on Earth

More Turkey Talk

Funky Chickens

Wicked World

DIFFERENCE

It would not be very good
If we had the **same colour,**
It would not be very good
If we all had the **same mother,**
It would not be very good
If we were from the **same place,**
It would not be very good
If we all had the **same face.**

It would not be very good
If we all wore the **same clothes,**
It would not be very good
And every smart kid knows
You're not even the same
As your sister or brother,
So it would not be very good
If we were **copies of each other.**

I don't want to get personal
Excuse me if I'm rude,
But it would not be very good
If we all ate the **same food,**
It would not be very good
If we all had the **same grin**
And it would not be very good
If we all liked the **same things.**

In my humble opinion
We have to learn to share
Because life would be quite strange
If we all had the **same hair,**
We should celebrate our differences
The world's full of different people,
But even though we're different

We can all be treated equal.

FOREWORD by George the Poet

I'm surprised that Benjamin Zephaniah became so famous. Usually people who speak out against the powerful don't become mainstream celebrities. But Benjamin was different; his words rose above any divides and brought people together. He didn't just talk about peace and pride and the struggle for justice – he lived his life by those principles, every single day.

You'll always see him described as a poet, an author, a playwright and an activist. But those words alone can't really capture everything he was. Lots of poets write poems, and lots of activists campaign for change. Rarely does one person to do it all, especially for as long as he did, creating so much important work that still resonates and feels relevant to this day.

My first introduction to Benjamin was through his funny, clever poem 'Talking Turkeys', which I found in my primary school library. Later, I discovered his novel *Gangsta Rap*, which I read just before I wrote *my* first ever rap verse. A coincidence? Maybe. Wherever I found his writing – whether at school or in my local Jamaican community – the message was always clear: **poetry is for everyone, and it can be about anything.**

One of the things he wrote a lot about was his hometown of Handsworth in Birmingham, celebrating its vibrancy and strength when others overlooked it. His powerful voice cut through the noise, calling out Britain's unfair treatment of the British Caribbean community and empowering many others in the process. You see, from the very start, Benjamin Zephaniah was committed to speaking up for the oppressed, the overlooked, the ignored. And as his career progressed, he never abandoned this important mission.

Benjamin's care for others also extended far beyond his own community. He spoke up for political prisoners, victims of war, animals – even the planet itself! But above all, his priority was children – all children, everywhere. This is partly why he kept his poetry so accessible; he wasn't writing to show off big words or to seem deep, he was writing to reach hearts and minds of all ages.

As a poet myself, people have often compared me to Benjamin Zephaniah. It's a huge honour, but as I learned more about all the things he achieved, it started to feel a bit much! We have some things in common: we are both part of a wave of Black British artists who have helped to change British culture – his medium was dub poetry, mine was rap music. We also both started writing when we were young, often about things that upset or angered us. But I like to go quiet and hold back most of what I write. Benjamin stayed vocal, regularly releasing new works and interacting with the world through his poems, books, plays and TV appearances – for decades!

Benjamin Zephaniah is my role model. Like him, I believe that poetry is for everyone. But I also know that beyond his writing, the man had a good heart. Like so many people, I found that whenever I spoke to him, he was patient, funny and generous with his advice. Benjamin didn't pretend to be perfect, nor did he pretend that the world was perfect, but in everything he did, he pushed for a better tomorrow. He stood up for what was right and used his ever-expanding influence not for selfish goals, but to represent the voiceless. I can only hope that future generations will celebrate his legacy and follow his example.

TALKING TURKEYS

GREET TINGS

Assalaam Alaikum
Hola
Szia
Sat Srii Akaal
Wa Happen
Zdravo
Yia Sou
Merhaba
Hej
Yo
Sawast Dee Craap
Ciao
Zdravstvuyte
Endemenesh
Ahoj
Bonjour
Yassou
Shalom
Namaste
Dag
Guten Tag
Buenos Dias
Parev
Ehida
Selamat Datong
Dia Dhuit
Hallo
And Welcome

BODY TALK

Dere's a Sonnet
Under me bonnet
Dere's a Epic
In me ear,
Dere's a Novel
In me navel
Dere's a Classic
Here somewhere.
Dere's a Movie
In me left knee
A long story
In me right,
Dere's a shorty
Inbetweeny
It is tickly
In de night.
Dere's a picture
In me ticker
Unmixed riddims
In me heart,
In me texture
Dere's a comma
In me fat chin
Dere is Art.

Dere's an Opera
In me bladder
A Ballad's
In me wrist
Dere is laughter
In me shoulder
In me guzzard's
A nice twist.
In me dreadlocks
Dere is syntax
A dance kicks
In me bum
Thru me blood tracks
Dere run true facts
I got limericks
From me Mum,
Documentaries
In me entries
Plays on history
In me folk,
Dere's a Trilogy
When I tink of three
On me toey
Dere's a joke.

RUNNING

I reckon I could run de world,
I used to run me school,
Hundred metres an two hundred metres,
I could run up Mount Everest
Wid a drink,
I could run tings wid big words
Like,
INFRASTRUCTURE,
an
TELECOMMUNICATION,
A marathon? Easy.
I could run out of bounds,
I run wild all de time
I run tings nice...as dey sey in Jamaica,
Or cool...as dey sey in Iceland,
I could run de Universe...in verse
But I haven't been given a chance.
I will get my chance,
Politicians are running outta ideas,
Dat may mean dat we all, you and me,
I an I,
All of we, may hav to run our own lives,
Dats bad...as dey sey in New York,
Way out...as dey sey in space,
All right...as dey sey in

FEAR NOT

Wanna be in our gang?
We cause Peace,
Fighters fear us,
On de streets
We shout slogans
Like,
Peace an Luv
One race, de Human Race
Make Patties Not War
An
Kiss a lip.

We are very safe
Animal friendly
Flower power crazy
Whole wheat flour fans.
We are de listening gang,
We want yu to say yes,
More,
Do it,
Go save everything.

Our only enemy is Ignorance
When we see it we rap it
In questions,
Reasoning an openmindedness,
We recycle ideas
An produce true stories,
Your stories,
Her stories an his stories,
Wid luv stories.

We hav no words for things
like,
Join us,
We luv yu baby
We luv yu people
We luv yu grasshopper.

LITTLE SISTER

That's my little sister
Just five minutes old
Already seeking something
To bite and chew and hold,
That's my little sister
Already going bald
I can't just call her sister
So what will she be called?

I want to call her Carol
But all carols are hymns
I want to call her Jimmy
But I always visit gyms,
I want to call her spotty
But she may punch my nose
I will not call her Rosy
She don't look like a rose.

When I hear her crying
I want to call her *loud*
If she's the type for talking
I may call her a *crowd*,
If she's good at singing
I'll call her *nightingale*
If she keeps on grinning
She'll make the doctors wail.

The doctors called her beauty
But beauty is a horse
The nurses called her cutey
Being polite of course,
My Mummy and my Daddy
Just don't have an idea
We don't have a name ready
But we're so glad she's here.

FRIENDS

Funky monkey in the tree
I like when you talk to me
What I really like the best
Is when you bang upon my chest.

Slippery snake I am your mate
When all others hesitate
I'll be there right by your side
I am known to slip and slide.

Hop along, croak croak, how ya doing **frog?**
No one understands our deep dialogue
People may laugh when they see us on the road
We must stick together
Monkey, snake, me, you and **toad**.

ACCORDING TO MY MOOD

I have ***poetic*** **licence,** i WriTe thE way i wa**Nt.**

i ***drop*** my **full stops** where ***i*** like **.** **.** **.**

MY CAPITAL Lete**R**s go where i li**KE**,

i **order** from **MY** PeN, i verse **the way** i like

(i do *my spelling write*)

Acording to My ***mo***od.

i **HA**ve **P**oetic **licence**,

i put my **commers** where **i** like,,**((O)).**

(((my brackets ***are*** **write**((

I REPEAT **WH**en i lik**E**.

i can't **go rong.**

i ***look*** and **i.e.**

It's rite.

i**I** REPEAT **WH**en i lik**E**.

i have *poetic* licence!

don't question me? ? ? ?

ROYAL TEA

I went to Buckingham Palace today
To see where the Queen and her family stay
I went to Buckingham Palace today
To see the Queen's horses and men,
The Queen had gone shopping
A friend let us in
A very big chap with a very big grin
He put all the money I had in a tin
Security checked me and then,
He showed me a picture three hundred years old
Kept in a frame made of valuable gold
I told him I had one just like it indoors
And that I may sell it to help a good cause,
A chandelier he said was priceless was nice
I said my one's better and it has a price
I went in a big room and saw a big throne
Just like the one my Mum has at home.

I saw carpets on walls that were not for sale
I met the man who sorts out royal mail
I went in the room where the Queen has her balls
And in there I saw some more carpets on walls,
On high polished floors I had a good slide
I got a good telling off from the guide
That very big chap with the very big grin
Now looked even bigger was not smiling,
I said in his ear that I needed to

Pay a quick visit to the royal loo
It took fifteen minutes to get myself there
Upon the loo door it said 'Kilroy waz ere'
Cameras filmed me on return to reception
I signed autographs for my royal connections
I left a note for the Queen saying she can
Visit me anytime she's in East Ham.

I went to Buckingham Palace today
To see where the Queen and her family stay
I went to Buckingham Palace today
To see royal things old and new,
It cost me eight fifty but no need to worry
If you visit me you don't need any money
There's no OBEs but there's fresh tea with honey
And I can take photos of **you**.

HOW'S DAT

No Sir
I don't play Cricket,
One time I try
Fearing a duck
I watch de ball fly towards me,
I recall every spin
An unforgettable air speed,
It bounced before me
Jus missing a two-day-old ant,
Up it cum
A red flash
Lick me finger so hard
I thought me finger would die.

Teacher tell me
I am good at cricket,
I tell teacher
I am not,
Teacher tell me
We love cricket,
I tell teacher
Not me,
I want Trigonometry
Fe help me people,
Teacher tell me
I am a born Cricketer,
But I never...well only once,
I don't play cricket.

VEGAN DELIGHT

Ackees, chapatties
Dumplins an nan,
Channa an rotis
Onion uttapam,
Masala dosa
Green callaloo
Bhel an samosa
Corn an aloo.
Yam an cassava
Pepperpot stew,
Rotlo an guava
Rice an tofu,
Puri, paratha
Sesame casserole,
Brown eggless pasta
An brown bread rolls.

Soya milked muesli
Soya bean curd,
Soya sweet sweeties
Soya's de word,
Soya bean margarine
Soya bean sauce,
What can mek medicine?
Soya of course.

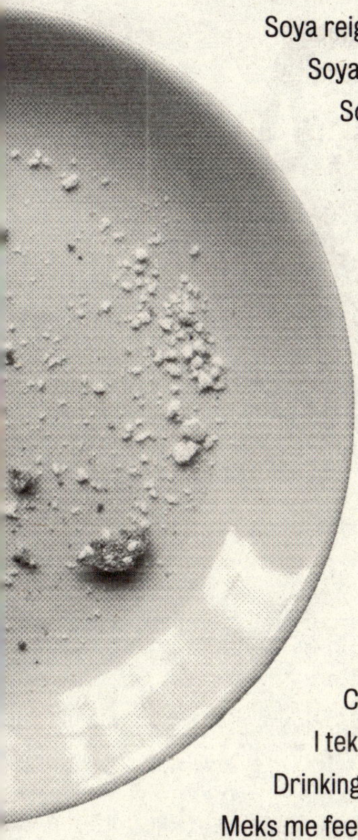

Soya meks yoghurt
Soya ice-cream,
Or soya sorbet
Soya reigns supreme,
Soya sticks liquoriced
Soya salads
Try any soya dish
Soya is bad.

Plantain an tabouli
Cornmeal pudding
Onion bhajee
Wid plenty cumin,
Breadfruit an coconuts
Molasses tea
Dairy free omelettes
Very chilli.
Ginger bread, nut roast
Sorrell, paw paw,
Cocoa an rye toast
I tek dem on tour,
Drinking cool maubi
Meks me feel sweet,
What was dat question now?
What do we eat?

OPEN MARKET

MULTI-CULTURE

I really luv chapatties
I eat dem all de time,
Today Iqbal made ten of dem
An nine of dem were mine,
I am krazy over mangoes
I once grew a mango tree,
My mango tree grew chapatties
Especially for me.

FOOD FOR THOUGHT

Fed up with your old dog food
Try new **'Johnny'**.
Johnny contains all the goodness your dog needs.
Ideal for weight watching dogs,
Bite size pieces means less chewing for doggy
Lots of juicy gravy means doggy gets a stiff drink
And a happy dog means you're happy.
Look,
When confronted with 'some other dog food'
Your dog may wag its tail,
With new **Johnny** tails go krazy
Ears flip flop
Everything goes shaky, shaky, shaky,
Guard dogs don't fear
Johnny is here,
At prices some people can afford.

We spoke to Mrs Pal, a top breeder,
She said
'Get lost',
Then we spoke to Mr P.Chum,
He said
'I like it, I like it'.
Try new **Johnny** from Bite and Barkers,
Dogs would chose **Johnny**,
Johnny tastes so good.

Bite and Barkers products are not tested on animals.

MR CANDYMAN

Candyman, Candyman
Give me a sweet
Sugar free
And carob coated
I deserve a treat
I've been working so hard
Counting all me toes
Looking at me garden
Watching how it grows.
Dear Mr Candyman
I don't have ten pence
But I may just sell dis poem
If it can make sense,
If I even sell one line
You can eat with me
Or we can buy a seed
And plant an apple tree.

Thanks Mr Candyman

It's a lovely colour
I think I may cut it in half
And share it with me brother,
If me brother likes it
He may just buy me poem
We're poor but we do part exchange
That's how we keep going.

A DAY IN THE LIFE OF DANNY THE CAT

Danny wakes up
Eats
Finds a private place in the garden,
He returns
Plays with the plants
And sleeps.
Danny wakes up
Eats
Inspects the garden
Finds a cosy place
And sleeps.
Danny wakes up
Comes indoors
Inspects the carpet
Scratches himself
And sleeps.
Danny wakes up
Goes in the garden
Over the fence
Has a fight with Ginger
Makes a date with Sandy
Climbs on to next door's shed
And sleeps.

Danny wakes up
Comes indoors
Rubs up the chair leg
Rubs up a human leg

Sharpens his claws
On a human leg
Eats
And sleeps.

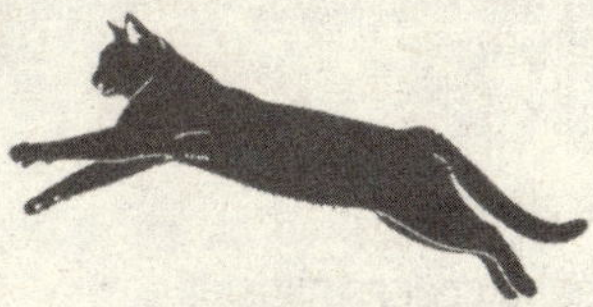

Danny wakes up
Eats
Watches a nature programme
Finds a private place in the
garden,

Finds Sandy in next door's garden
Next door's dog finds Danny

Sandy runs north
Danny runs home
Eats an sleeps.

Danny wakes up
Checks for mice
Checks for birds
Checks for dogs
Checks for food
Finds a private place in the garden
Eats
And sleeps.

Danny has hobbies,
Being stroked
Car watching
And smelling feet
He loves life,
Keeps fit
And keeps clean,
Every night he covers himself
In spit,
Then he eats
And sleeps.

DRIVOSAURUS REX

The dinosaurs are back
Working at Hollywood
Now they are not flesh and bone
They're plastic, foam and wood
The dinosaurs are here
I saw one on a bus
As I was on the way to play
At Dinosaurs 'R' Us.

They came from Noah's Ark
Unto Jurassic Park
When they ete you can bet
They did some great big
Barks,
Then from Jurassic Park
Some came into our homes
In big boxes of cereals
With added rocks and stones.

The dinosaurs are back
With bottom, front and side
The ones I've seen look kind of mean
And really very wide,
These dinosaurs are stars
I've seen them on radars
Looking cool and deadly
As they drive around in cars.

PART WAN

I wonder how babies are made,
All babies
Homosapien babies,
Donkey babies,
Bird babies.
Animals kiss
An den what
Babies.
Dere mus be more to it.

PART TWO

Life has its ups an downs
Even captives smile
I wonder why people die?
Dere mus be more to it.

WORDOLOGY

Sociologists

Physicists

Archacologists

And

Anthropologists

Like

Dieticians

Rhetoricians

Mathematicians

And

Politicians

Are simple people,

Help them.

DE GENERATION RAP

Dat guy **BAD**
He's ***kicking,***
He's ***wicked,***
CRUCIAL,
Cums round *here*
Wida **smiley** pon his face,
He CHILLS out,
Slides round,
Mekni circles,
He's **safe.**

Dis sista hard
She's ***irie***,
MENTAL
RESPECT due,
She steps ***cool***
Trods ***easy***,
Hang **tuff,**
BIG UP
An ***vitalistic.***

When him pass thru
HARD VIBES,
Him ***wild***,
Is a **neat** dude
SLICK geeza
A ***natural*** bro.
Made **up.**
She jus **oow,**
Streetwise G,
She's covered
Fit, Irie,
X.

People on de **streets**
Luv dem so much,
Dem **jus call** dem
***Drr* R*ead* *fu*ll.**

SOLIDARITY

An army of militant greens
In bio-degradable genes
Shout **'Give peas a chance
An lettuce all dance
In unity wid butter beans'.**

MEDIEVAL RELIGIOUS TRIBAL CHANT

HERE WE GO

HERE WE GO

HERE WE GO

(Please repeat)

WHO'S WHO

I used to think **nurses**
Were women,
I used to think **police**
Were men,
I used to think **poets**
Were boring,
Until **I** became **one of them.**

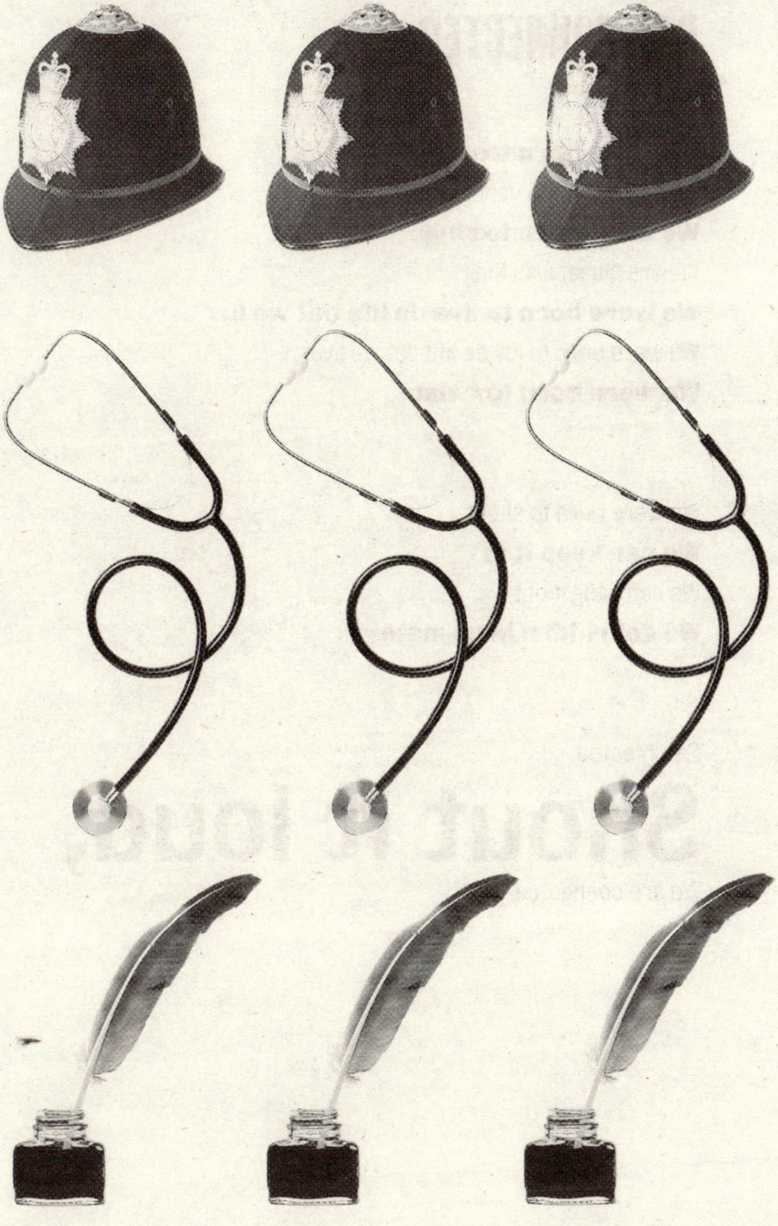

RAP CONNECTED

We were born to rap
We were born to dance
We were born to sing
We are Queens an Kings
We were born to live de life dat we luv
We were born to luv de life dat we live,
We were born to twist

We were born to shout
We can keep it in
We can hang it out
We got riddim in us mate

Get infected,
Shout it loud,
We are connected.

We were born to share
An hav fun whilst here,
So if you don't care
Go somewhere you square,
If you are aware
You will be respected
We all share the air and
We are connected.

We are black an brown
We are white an sound
We have pride of place
We are on de case
We are wild an tame
We are all de same

Sister, brother, kid,
We are connected.

A KILLER LIES

He's a Fox Hunter, he said
'Foxes need controlling, they spread germs
They're always mating.'
I think he's exaggerating,
He's a Fox Hunter, he said
'They're wild animals, they eat lambs and they eat chickens.'
He needs chickens for his kitchen.

He calls foxes beast,
But he collects their teeth,
He kills thousands every year
Once he whispered in me ear,
'It will kill you with its bite
That is why fox hunting's right,
Can't you sense they are evil
So unlike hunting people,
They are the enemy of our community
I love it when they're caught
And they make such good sport,
I never tasted one
When our hounds get them they're gone,
I am good at this you know
I'm a kind of Hunt hero.'

He's a Fox Hunter
His Daddy taught him well
When his hounds scent de smell
Excitement meks him yell,
He's a Fox Hunter
Know him by his killer eyes
Something dead must be his prize
He's de kind dat's **civilized.**

HEROES

Heroes are funny people, dey are lost an found
Sum heroes are brainy an sum are muscle-bound,
Plenty heroes die poor an are heroes after dying
Sum heroes mek yu smile when yu feel like crying.
Sum heroes are made heroes as a political trick
Sum heroes are sensible an sum are very thick!
Sum heroes are not heroes cause dey do not play de game
A hero can be young or old and have a silly name.
Drunks an sober types alike hav heroes of dere kind
Most heroes are heroes out of sight an out of mind,
Sum heroes shine a light upon a place where darkness fell
Yu could be a hero soon, yes, yu can never tell.
So if yu see a hero, better treat dem wid respect
Poets an painters say heroes are a prime subject,
Most people hav heroes even though some don't admit
I say we're all heroes if we do our little bit.

BEYOND DE BELL

Yu push
Yu shove
Believing
School moves round **yu**,
Yu spy an lie
Believing
Tings control by **yu**,
What mek **yu** tink like dat?
Never mind
Academic ability
Concentration span
I.Q. business
Yu big in de playground,
Never mind
People who
Don't push an shove,
Yu do.

Table may turn
Yu may be pushed,
An macho boy
Yu may lose **yu** watch
Yu ill gained sweet money
Yu bigheadedness,
Table may turn
Yu may be shoved
Den walked over
By an army
Of carers

Teaching lessons,
We don't want dat now
Do we.

Yu are not respected
Yu are other tings,
People do talk behind **yu** back
Whatever **yu** say,
We all have problems
But
Dere are people who will talk to **yu**
If **yu** won't talk to yuself.

Yu grab an slap
An won't give back
Believing
It's over at four,
By day yu taunt
At night yu haunt,
Believing
Yu rule OK,
What mek yu tink like dat?
Is it
Parents,
Dreams,
Bigger bullies
Or television,
Who do we blame,
An
What mek yu tink like dat?

CIVIL LIES

Dear Teacher,

When I was born in Ethiopia
Life began,
As I sailed down the Nile civilization began,
When I stopped to think universities were built,
When I set sail
Asians and true Americans sailed with me.

When we traded nations were built,
We did not have animals,
Animals lived with us,
We had so much time
Thirteen months made our year,
We created social services
And cities that still stand.

So teacher do not say
Columbus discovered me
Check the great things I was doing
Before I suffered slavery.

Yours truly,
Mr Africa

POEMS FROM THE LAST PERSON ON EARTH

FOR SALE

Looking for a bargain
Come on down
It's the Sale of the Century
Look around
There are sights to see
And places to be
With way out cosmic activity
This is a deal that you can't refuse
The kind of bet you cannot lose
So come on down
The price is right
I got to sell this thing tonight.

Chorus

Roll up, Roll up, Planet for Sale
Roll up, Planet for Sale.

Free of living things that roam
Free of people and ozone
I invite you to test my ware
Free of any atmosphere
Enjoy yourself as you get poorly
With no sign of a creepy crawly
I promise you will find no trees

And no flowers to make you sneeze.
Little Bo Peep has gone with her sheep
And little Jack Horner dissolved in a corner,
That Donald Duck has run out of luck
And Paddington Bear is no longer here
The Owl and the Pussy Cat went to sea
Then got lost in infinity.
Alive Alive no, Alive Alive no
Cockles and Mussels are not,
And no snow.

Chorus

Roll up, Roll up, Planet for Sale
Roll up, Planet for Sale.

Looking for a bargain, check this planet
Not a thing is moving on it
Just for you I'll do a deal
I'll swap it for a decent meal.

A BEETLE CALLED DEREK

There once was a Beetle called Derek
Who lived in a forest on Earth
And this little Beetle called Derek
Was really attracted to dirt,
She did not carry no weapons
Except what she naturally got
She did not have no possessions
But she could look after her lot.

The forest protected our Derek
Predators came and they went,
This was no reason to panic
Cause this was with Nature's consent,
She was related to Wind and Fire
A sister of necessity,
She was related to Earth and Water
A distant cousin to me.
Doctors could not work out Derek
Derek had secrets she kept,
Then came the white coated bandits
Scientists seeking all they could get,
Her home was robbed to make paper
And that got the climate upset,
Cows would graze to make burgers
The cows never made a profit!!

Derek was taken for granted
By selfish, non-beetle people,
Some supporters of Derek demanded
An end to what we called Evil,
Handouts could not solve the problem alone
So I called out the Eco-Police,
But we could not win the fight on our own
Now Derek my friend is deceased.

There once was a Beetle called Derek
Who lived in a forest on Earth,
Nobody knew where she came from
A kind of mysterious birth,
I built a memorial to Derek
Hoping that it may be seen,
I hope when I die I'll see Derek,
In a heaven organic and green.

BEAT IT

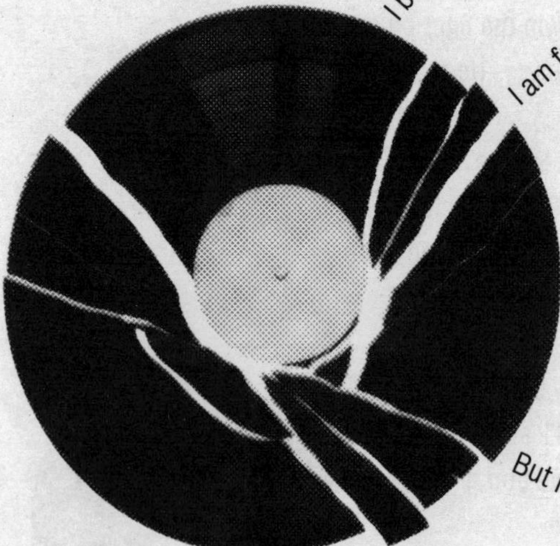

I broke my world record
I am famous for it
But now I am so bored
Cos I have no music.

PETS CONTROL

We moved into a house
We kicked de animals out,
Den we got our pets
An signed on at de vets,
We den called wild life strays
Zoos captured dem,
We gazed,
Wild life made great TV,
How civilized were we?

MEMORIES

I recall a time
Not long ago
When sheep would roam around here,
If you were nice and friendly
You could get close to a deer,
Foxes, rabbits
Wild and free
We had so much potential,
But we did not live in harmony
And that was detrimental.
I take no blame
I did not do it
I was an innocent child,
My roots are very vegan
I like my animals wild,
I take no blame
I did not do it
I wrote to all the rulers,
I took a stand,
I loved the land
How I loved the Animal Kingdom.

I saw people training dogs
To make the doggies violent
Rulers of the land made dog owners
Buy a licence,
I saw furs of animals
Upon human backs
I saw furs of animals
Being used as mats,
It happened here, I saw it
I called it Human Madness
I saw friends disappear
Imagine all my sadness,
I shouted from all high places
Let us not do this crime,
Nobody listened to me
Nobody had the time.

Memories don't leave like people do
I miss the kangaroo,
I recall great big trees,
I need these memories.

THINK ME

I want to be
In someone's mind

For ever

And ever

All right,

I want my picture taken
I must be someone's thought,
Somebody somewhere
Dream of me
I want to be
REMEMBERED.

MORE TURKEY TALK

I

If
Big
Boys
Don’t
Cry
‘
‘
Why
Do
I
?
.

LETTERS

I keep reading luv letters
So I won’t feel alone,
I’ll publish it an frame it
If I get one of me own.

KISS AN TELL

I kissed a girl
She nicked me tongue
It swept me off me feet,
It blew de air from out me lungs
An me heart missed a beat
Me liver quivered
Me legs shivered
Me head started swelling
Me eyes rolled back
Me back went crack
Den she started yelling,

'Clean your teeth!'

OVER DE MOON

Dere's a man on de moon
He's skipping an stuff,
Dere's a man on de moon
He looks very tuff,
Dere's a man on de moon
An he's all alone,
Dere's a man on de moon
His wife is at home.

He's dancing around
To real moony music,
He carries his air
He knows how to use it,
He waves to his wife
Still on Planet E,
She's waving back
But he cannot see.

De man on de moon is so clever,
He has sum ideas to persue,
His chewing gum can last fe ever
His fast food is already chewed.

Dere's a man on de moon
He has a spaceship,
Dere's a man on de moon
An we payed fe it,
Dere's a man on de moon
His mission ain't done,
Dere's a man on de moon
He's after de Sun.

MOVIE MADNESS

Jellybean one waz a blockbuster
Jellybean two waz a flop
Jellybean three a disaster
Jellybean four cost a lot
Jellybean five waz a miss take
Jellybean six was withdrawn
Jellybean seven a headache
Jellybean eight made us yawn.
Jellybean nine was just too much
Jellybean ten came and went
Jellybean films made me bankrupt
Because my film money's all spent.

FAIR PLAY

Mirror mirror on the wall
Could you please return our ball
Our football went through your crack
You have two now
Give one back.

JUDE

Dere waz a cool dude called Jude
Who waz terribly awfully rude,
She spread bubble gum
All over her bum
An now she is
stuck in de nude.

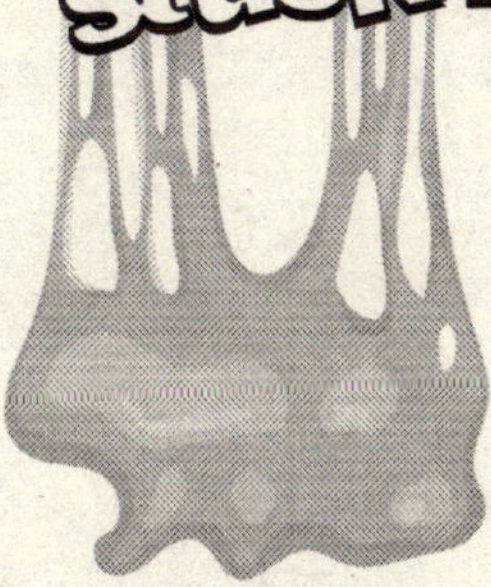

TELLING OFF

Get your feet from **off** that table
Get your hands **out** of that pie
Get your teeth **out** of that apple
Get your things and say **goodbye**.

LUV SONG

I am in luv wid a hedgehog
I've never felt dis way before
I have luv fe dis hedgehog
An everyday I luv her more an more,
She lives by de shed
Where weeds an roses bed
An I just want de world to know
She makes me glow.

I am in luv wid a hedgehog
She's making me hair stand on edge,
So in luv wid dis hedgehog
An her friends
Who all live in de hedge
She visits me late
An eats off Danny's plate
But Danny's a cool tabby cat
He leaves it at dat.

I am in luv wid a hedgehog,
She's gone away so I must wait
But I do miss my hedgehog
Everytime she goes to hibernate.

EYE SEE?

I've never seen flowers fight

It seems

Not all living things do,

I've never seen poodles get dr

Many well dressed,

I have seen elephants fly

It seems Not all people see what I see,

I've never seen a blind person lost

It seems **Only the sighted lose their way**

REMEMBRANCE DAYS

Ramadan in Pakistan
Is a special time
On Christmas Day in
Jamaica
The sun will always shine,
Diwali in India
Brings all the colours out
And don't forget
In Tibet
Each day
A Poet
Shouts.

EVERYDAY

Happy Birthday.
Today
You
Are
One
Day
Older,
Let's celebrate.

TALKING TURKEYS!!

Be nice to yu turkeys dis christmas
Cos turkeys jus wanna hav fun
Turkeys are cool, turkeys are wicked
An every turkey has a Mum.
Be nice to yu turkeys dis christmas,
Don't eat it, keep it alive,
It could be yu mate an not on yu plate
Say, Yo! Turkey I'm on your side.

I got lots of friends who are turkeys
An all of dem fear christmas time,
Dey wanna enjoy it, dey say humans destroyed it
An humans are out of dere mind,
Yeah, I got lots of friends who are turkeys
Dey all hav a right to a life,
Not to be caged up an genetically made up
By any farmer an his wife.

Turkeys jus wanna play reggae
Turkeys jus wanna hip-hop
Can yu imagine a nice young turkey saying,
'I cannot wait for de chop'?
Turkeys like getting presents, dey wanna watch christmas TV,
Turkeys hav brains an turkeys feel pain
In many ways like yu an me.

I once knew a turkey called
Turkey
He said 'Benji explain to me please,
Who put de turkey in christmas
An what happens to christmas trees?'
I said, 'I am not too sure turkey
But it's nothing to do wid Christ Mass
Humans get greedy an waste more dan need be
An business men mek loadsa cash.'

Be nice to yu turkey dis christmas
Invite dem indoors fe sum greens
Let dem eat cake an let dem partake
In a plate of organic grown beans,
Be nice to yu turkey dis christmas
An spare dem de cut of de knife,
Join Turkeys United an dey'll be delighted
An yu will mek new friends **'FOR LIFE'.**

CHRISTMAS WISE

All I **want** fe christmas is world peace
I **don't want** loads a food dat I really can't eat
All I **want** fe christmas is a long holiday
An a house in Jamaica where I can stay.
I **don't want** kisses under mistletoe from
Sloppy people I don't know,
I **won't** be putting out nu stocking cos
I **don't** wear de tings,
I **won't** be cutting down nu christmas trees,
I like dem living.

All I **want** fe christmas is dis planet for ever
Fully complete wid its ozone layer
All I **want** fe christmas is friends and...
No more records from Status Quo,
I **don't want** a white christmas an I bet
We'll get nu more of dem cos of de Greenhouse effect,
An I **reckon** at christmas we create too much waste
Maybe a green christmas is more to my taste.
All I **want** fe christmas is sum honesty
About de wisdom of christmas
An how it should be
All I **want** fe christmas is clean air,
But I reckon I won't get none
An I don't think dat's fair.

SUNNYSIDE UP

When people
See people
Reading up
Side down,
They think,
Maybe,
The reader
Can't read,
But
You should
Smile now,
Because you
Have found
A poem
That's out
To mislead.

ONCE UPON A TIME

I dreamt of living in a great big house
With a great big cat and a great big mouse
With a great big cupboard
Full of great big pears
I would grow great big
Without any cares.
Me great big hair on me great big head
Would feel great tucked into
Me great big bed
In me great bedroom
I would have great fights
With me big shadow
Who is really bright,
A great big sun shine would wake me up
I would drink great juice from a great big cup
And a great breakfast would make me feel great
And me school teachers would be always late.

I would speak great poems
With me great big voice
Great big hugs and kisses
Would make me feel nice
This great world would work together as a team
I would live for ever
In me great big dream.

FUNKY
CHICKENS

NATURAL ANTHEM

God save our gracious green
Long live our glorious scene
God save our green.

Dis ting is serious
Do it for all of us
Save our asparagus,
God save
Our
Green.

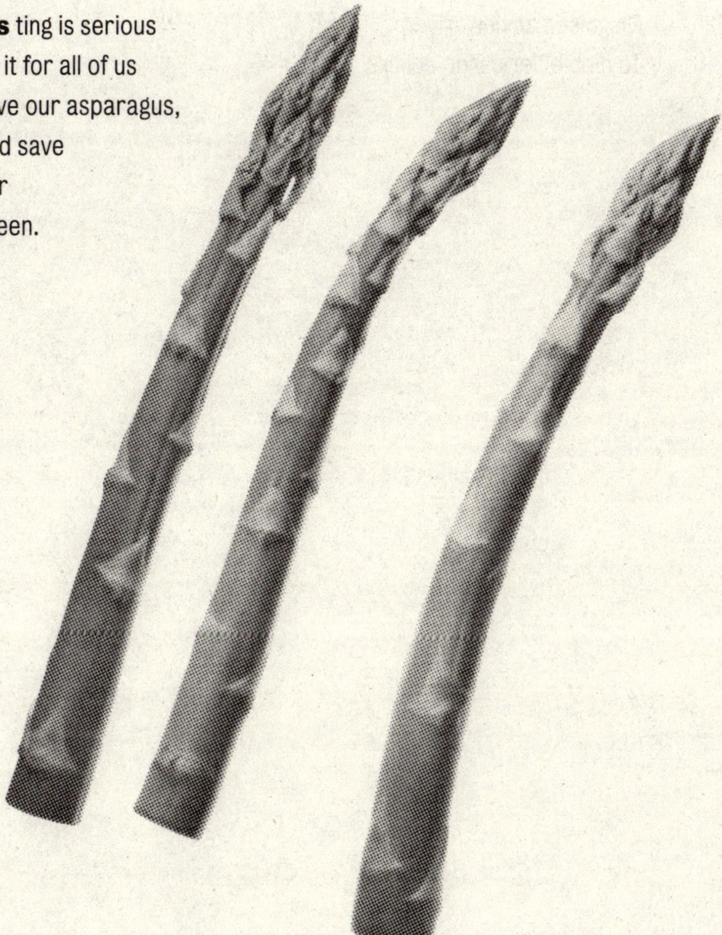

HEALTH FOOD STOP

Little Miss Muffet
Sat on her tuffet
Eating her organic pears,
Along came a spider
Disguised as her driver
To nibble her carob éclairs.

YORK'S SCHOOL REPORT

The Grand Old Duke of York
He could not count to **ten**,
When he got to **four** and a half
He had to start again,
On exam day he started at **none**
And he slowly progressed to **one**,
By the time he got **two**, **three** and **four**
His memory

had

gone.

FOR WORD

Thank you for the *words* I read
Thank you for the **words** I need
Thank you for the **WORDS** so great
Thanks for **words** that raise debate,
Thanks for the **words** on my bookshelf
Thanx for the **words** I make myself
Thank you for **words** that make me cry
And **words** that leave me feeling dry.

Thanks for **WORDS** that do inspire
And those **words** that burn like fire
Thanks for all the **words** I note
Thank you for all the **words** I quote,
I thank you for the **words** like me
Thanks for **WORDS** that set me free
And I thank you for **words** like you
I always need a **word** or two.

Thanks for **words** that make things plain
And **words** that help me to explain
Thanks for **words** that make life fun
And **words** that help me overcome,
Thanks for **words** that make me rap
Thanks for **words** that make me clap
Thanks for **WORDS** that make me smile
Thanks for **WORDS** with grace and style.

Thanks for all those **words** that sing
Thanks for **words** are everything
Thanks for all the **WORDS** like this
And little sloppy **words** like kiss,
Thanks for **words** like hip-hooray
And those cool **words** I like to say
Thanks for **words** that reach and touch
Thank you very, very much.

LIBRARY OLOGY

I have a date with Su Ling Lee
We're meeting at the library
At 5 o'clock by history
I'll show her some myth*ology*,
And if we have the energy
We'll check out some the*ology*
And if there is good chemistry
We'll dance by music*ology*.

We'll sail through ocean*ology*
And get some cool lith*ology*
And roundabout psych*ology*
I'll sweet talk her top*ology*,
With science and techn*ology*
We'll have some soci*ology*
And touch each others botany
With organic homoeopathy.

She knows so much cosm*ology*
I do luv her ec*ology*
And reading her astr*ology*
I note she has anatomy,
I'll use my best phrase*ology*
To get her to phon*ology*
So we can lexic*ology*
Together in the library.

SERIOUS LUV

Monday Morning

I really luv de girl dat's sitting next to me
I think she thinks like me an she's so cool,
I think dat we could live for ever happily
I want to marry her when I leave school.

She's de only one in school allowed to call me Ben
When she does Maths I luv de way she chews her pen,
When we are doing Art she's so artistic
In Biology she makes me heart beat so quick.

When we do Geography I go to paradise
She's helped me draw a map of Borneo twice!
Today she's going to help me take me books home
So I am going to propose to her when we're alone.

The next day

I used to luv de girl dat's sitting next to me
But yesterday it all came to an end,
She said that I should take love more seriously
An now I think I really luv her friend.

JELLYVISION

Daddy's on de telly
Showing off his belly
He wants to be a star
But he's not getting far,
He tried to read de weather
He really did endeavour
But he's really not dat clever
He made no sense whatsoever.

Daddy's on de box
Squeezing all his spots
He wants to read de news
But he only knows de blues,
He's tried to do a trick
Wid a rabbit an a stick
But de rabbit waz too slick
An me Daddy's not too quick.

I know you don't believe me
But Daddy's on de TV
He's doing a commercial
Dat's very controversial,
He's trying to sell hair spray
Dat stops hair going grey
Which haz extra dirty clay
They should lock Daddy away.

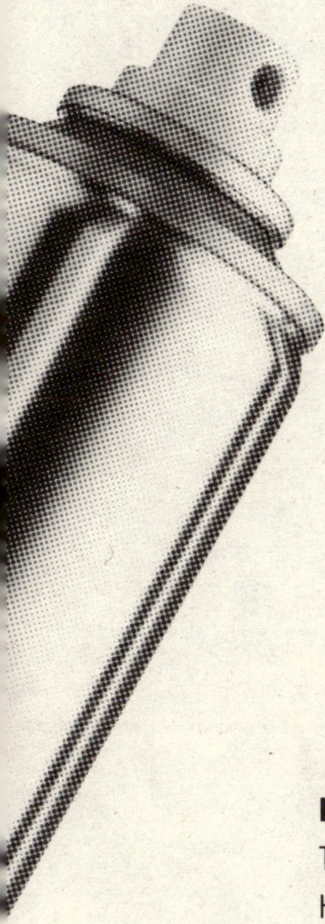

Daddy did not get permission
To go on de television
He thinks life will be easier
Working in de media,
But I don't think he's ready
He just does not look steady
He's shivering like jelly
Standing on de telly.

THE BUSKER

She strums upon the guitar
Like a rainbow strums the sky,
Her fingers sing a song
Upon the strings,
She brings to me old memories
Of a reggae lullaby,
And all the histories
That good reggae brings.

As I receive fine tuning
My hard times drift away,
My income tax bills
Weigh me down no more,
East Ham is full of fountains
Vibrations have their say
And all my ills receive
An instant cure.

Her music making makes me
A very gentle man
The melody is making
Common sense,
The passers by are busy
Making millions
And all I have to give
Is twenty pence.

BIRTHRIGHTS

Baby *is* a SUPERSTAR
She really **luvs** de stage
She's **HOT**
She's ***cool***
Yu **cannot** guess her **age**,
Baby *is* a SUPERSTAR
Don't tell ***her*** wot to do
She's **Safe**
She's **GREAT**
She's very much ***like you***.
Baby *is* a SUPERSTAR
So tek a picture ***quick***
She ***shines***
She's fine
So very ***poetic***,
Baby *is* a SUPERSTAR
She **sings**, she **plays**, she *writes*
Let's **listen** to her freedom songs
She's in ***concert*** tonight.

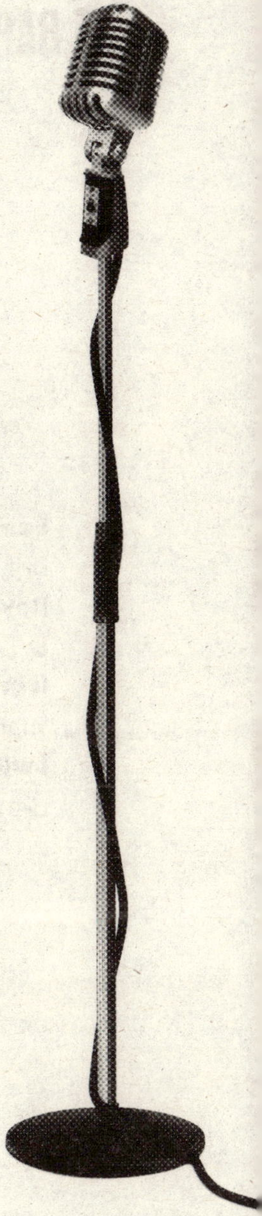

I DE RAP GUY

I am de rapping rasta
I rap de lyrics fasta
Dan a Ford Cortina
Or a double ghetto blasta,
When royals are listening
They proclaim me as a king
I am way out an travelling
Not a puppet on a string.

I am de rapping rasta
De lyrical masta
Dey say I am good to go
So I go wid de flow,
If yu really want to know
Yu should book me for a show
I will tek yu high an low
Like an eagle or a roe.

What I spread is unity
Or to put it simply
I want racial harmony
In de world community,
I am big an I am bad
So bad I will mek yu glad
An you'll hav to tell ya Dad
Bout de rapper yu just had.

I rap on de move
Wid a little tongue an groove
Wid ability to soothe
Warmongers may not approve,
I can put yu in your place
Wid a little drum an bass
I am proud of every race
I out ran de steeplechase.

I am de rapping rasta
Flesh an bone not plaster
My ideas are very green
An I keep me rapping clean,
Let me take you on a tour
I know what I'm rapping for,
I can rap from coast to coast
An I don't like to brag or boast.

IF YU SEE

IF yu see a zebra crossing
Stop an let it cross
If yu see a flower flowing
Let it flow,
If yu see someone who's bossy
Tell dem who's boss,
If yu see someone wid knowledge
Let dem know.

IF YU HEAR

IF yu hear some Rock an Roll
Try to rock an roll
If yu hear a rumour spreading

Mek sum room,

If yu hear a mole
Trying to dig a hole
Yu hav heard
A very dirty little tune.

POETICS

There's a poem on your face
There's a poem in the sky
There's a poem in outta space
There are poems passing by,
There are poems in your dreams
There are poems in your head
Sometimes I cannot get to sleep
Cause there are poems in me bed.

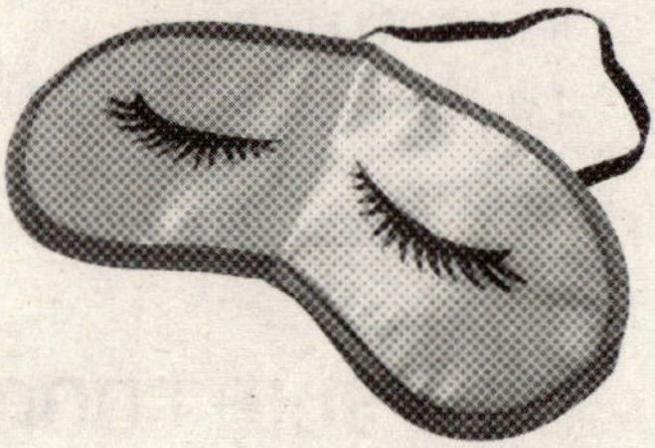

There are poems in me tea
There are poems on me toast
I have found much poetry
In the place I love the most,
There's a poem right in front of you
Get to know its rhyme,
If you are not sure what to do
Just call it poem time.

There's a poem in me shoes
There's a poem in me shirt
When the poem meets the blues
It can really, really hurt,
Other poems make you grin
When they dribble off your chin
Some poems think they are great
So they like to make you ...

Wait
I see poems in your teeth
I see poems in me cat
I hear poems underneath
Going rata tat tat tat,
This one has not finished yet
It keeps coming on the beat
It is soggy and it's wet
But it's also very sweet.

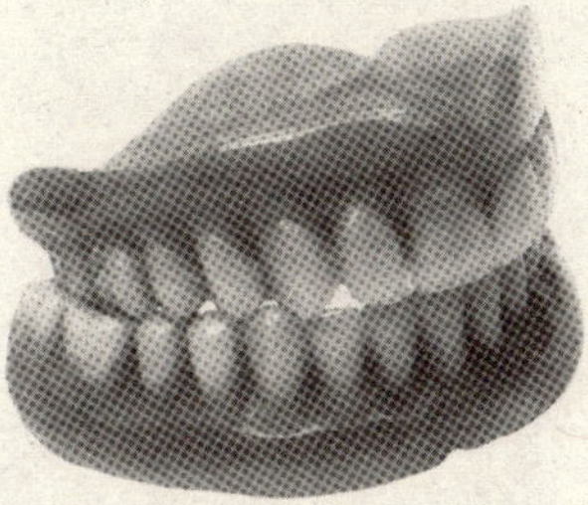

There are poems for the **ear**
There are poems for the page
Some poems are not quite clear
But they get better with age,
There are poems for the hip
There are poems for the hop
Everything is poetic
Poetry will never stop.

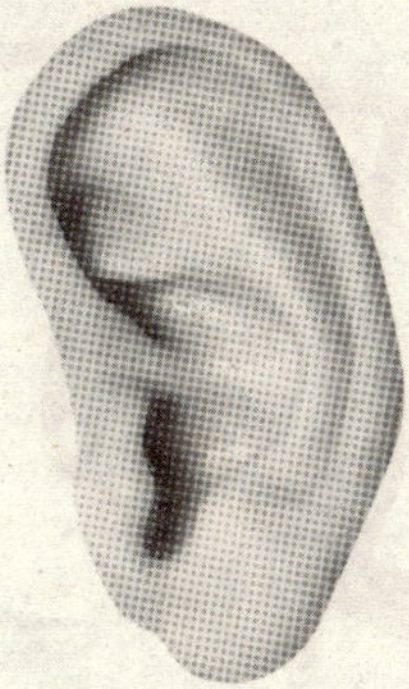

There are poems on your **fingers**
There's a poem on your nose
If you give it time to linger
It will grow and grow and grow,
There's a poem in you beautiful
Can't you see it
It's right

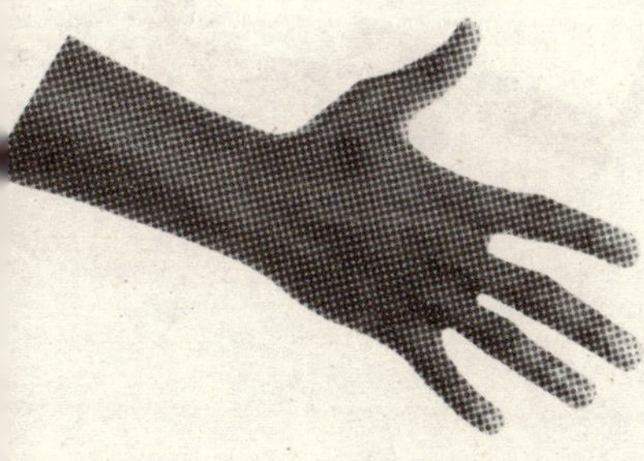

There,
I think it's so incredible
There are poems
Everywhere.

EPIC

My favourite poem started

EP

It will be a long one

A single line ago,

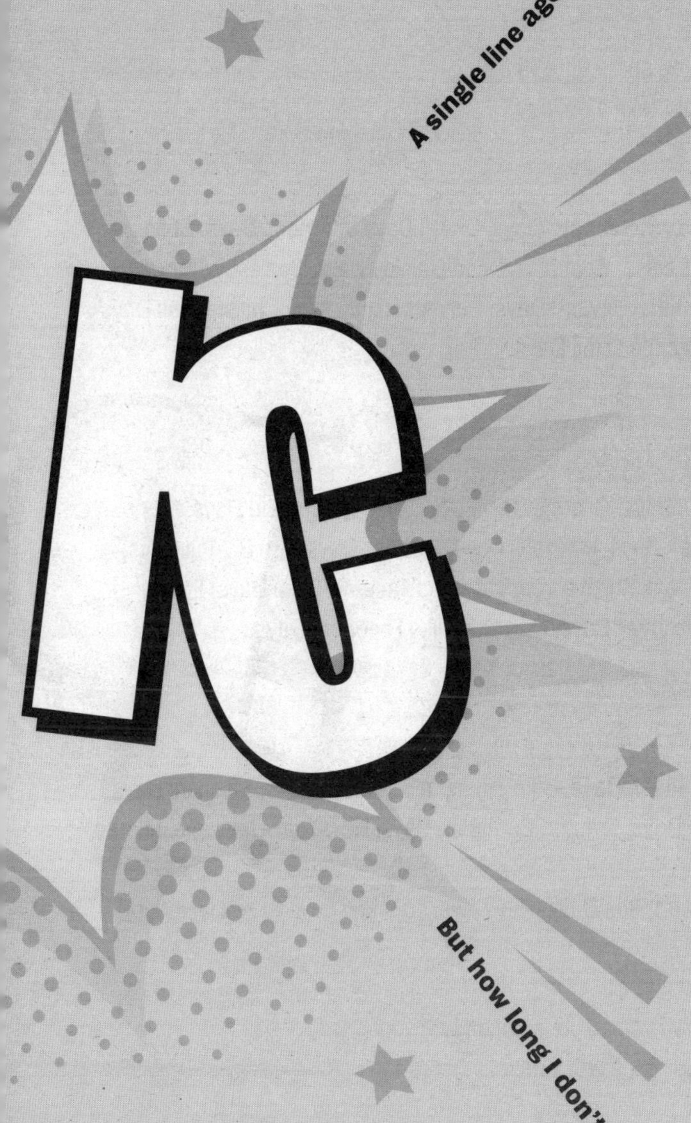

But how long I don't know.

PLAY DAZE

If you need some time to play
You should take a holiday
There are:

Birthdays, Sabbath Days, Diwali Days and Hero Days, Solstice
Days, Isis Days, Bodhi Days and Garvey Days, Sun Days, Moon
Days, Mahavir Jayanti Days, Burns's Night Days, Christ Mass Days
and days called Holi Days.

Or

Whit Sundays, Orange Days, Good Fridays and Eid Days,
Gahambar Days, Mothers Days, Fathers Days with Boxing Days,
Adonia Days, Shrove Tuesdays and Tang-no-Seku Days, Easter
Days, Passover Days, May Days like Freedom Days.

Try

Lion of Judah Days, Chin Yeung and Tin Hau Days, Vaishkhi Days,
Wedding Days, Kut and Ramadan Days, New Year Days, Geshi
Days,
Kathina and Rice Days, Hay Days, so many days to really get you
in a daze.

When you've had your holidays
You should try a work day.

BIRTHDAYS **EVERYBODY** • SABBATH **JEWISH** • DIWALI **HINDU**

HEROES DAYS **EVERYWHERE** • SOLSTICE **PAGAN** • ISIS **ANCIENT EGYPT**

BODHI **BUDDHIST** • GARVEY **RASTAFARIAN** • SUN DAYS **TRADITIONAL**

MOON DAYS **TRADITIONAL** • MAHAVIR JAYANTI **JAIN**

BURNS'S NIGHT **SCOTTISH TRADITION** • CHRISTMAS **CHRISTIAN**

HOLI **HINDU** • WHIT SUNDAY **CHRISTIAN** • ORANGE **CHRISTIAN**

GOOD FRIDAY **CHRISTIAN** • EID **MUSLIM** • GAHAMBAR **ZOROASTRIAN**

MOTHERS DAY **TRADITIONAL** • FATHERS DAY **TRADITIONAL**

BOXING DAY **CHRISTIAN** • ADONIA **ANCIENT GREEK**

SHROVE TUESDAY **CHRISTIAN** • TANG-NO-SEKU **JAPANESE TRADITION**

EASTER **CHRISTIAN** • PASSOVER **JEWISH** • MAY DAY **WORKERS / INTERNATIONAL**

FREEDOM DAY **POLITICAL/ INTERNATIONAL** • LION OF JUDAH **RASTAFARIAN**

CHIN YEUNG **BUDDHIST** • TIN HAU **BUDDHIST** • VAISHKHI **SIKH**

WEDDING DAY **EVERYWHERE** • KUT **KOREAN** • RAMADAN **MUSLIM**

NEW YEAR **EVERYWHERE** • GESHI **JAPANESE** •

KATHINA **BUDDHIST RICE AFRICAN - CARIBBEAN / ASIAN TRADITIONAL**

HAY **AFRICAN-CARIBBEAN/ASIAN TRADITIONAL** •

WORK DAY **EVERY DAY/EVERYWHERE**

THOUGHT FOR MONDAY

Why do people
Complain about Mondays,
Why do
People have
Monday morning blues
And that Monday morning feeling.
Monday is like any other day.

I think
People who suffer Monday morning blues
Read too many Sunday papers.

NOBODY DE GREAT

Nobody is king of de jungle
Nobody rules over de sea,
Nobody is great
Nobody's my mate,
Cause dere ain't nobody
But me.

DE RONG SONG

Your house is
Falling down
Around
Your
Feet,
And you got
Nought
To eat,
Don't worry
Be happy.

Your fish
Have drowned
You wear
A frown,
You search
But you don't
Own a pound,
Don't worry
Be happy.

You ain't got
Nowhere to
Play,
Just balconies
And
Motorways,
Don't
worry
Be happy.

You meet
Someone
You really like,
They tell you to
Get on your bike,
Don't worry
Be happy.

You're on your bike
And all is fine,
You get caught
In a washing line,
Don't worry
Be happy.

You go to school
The school is
Gone,
The Government
Put pressure on,
Don't worry
Be happy.

Your tea is
Dry
Your ice is
Hot,
Your head is
Tied up in a
Not,
Don't worry
Be happy.

You worry
Because
You're hurrying,
And hurry
Because
You're worrying,
Don't happy
Be worried.

ONLY ME

Me I am the oldest
On a young lad's quest
I am the worst at everything
And I am the best,
Yes I am the richest
I am very poor
I only need a little
But I must get some more.

My lifespan is the longest
Really it is short
I fought so hard for freedom
And now I have been caught,
I think I own this planet
I think that I am strong
I have to drop this habit
Of never being wrong.

I am the kind of teacher
Who has much to learn
The straight forward leader
Who has got to turn,
Call me Mr. President
Or call me the people,
The tutor or the student,
Because I am more equal.

I am looking at me
Looking at myself
I can see quite clearly
Me and no one else,
No one else reminds me
Of all that I so fear
Like being very lonely
And that is why I am here.

DE MAGIC POEM

I seek de magic poem
De one dat all de poets seek
I'm told dat it can ease our sorrows
An good harvest reap.
I seek de magic poem
In every language it can speak
It's celebrating our tomorrows
An it never sleeps.

I seek de magic poem
I know it's safe
I know it's good
I'm told dat it is full of light
I need it for me neighbourhood.

I seek de magic poem
I seek it high
I seek it low,
I'm told dat it is out of sight
Another poem told me so.

I seek de magic poem
Over de seas
Over de land
I'm at de ever ready
Try an overstand.

I seek de magic poem
It's in de mind
It's in de skies
I don't want to get heavy but
Dis poem never lies.

I seek de magic poem
De one de Pop Stars cannot sing
I'm told it will bring us music
A peace place create,
I seek de magic poem
Dat poem keeps me wondering
I'm told it's pure, true an organic
Dis hide an seek is great.

GOOD COMPANY

De Queen haz a poet
I think he's very odd,
De Priest haz a poet
I think his poet's God.
De Singer haz a poet
To help de singer sing,
And de Poet haz a poet
To keep him poeting.

THIS ORANGE TREE

I touched my first rose
Under this orange tree,
I was young and fruity
The sweet rose was blooming.

I found faith
Under this orange tree
It was here all the time,
One day I picked it up
Then I realized
How great you are.

It was under this
Very orange tree
That I read
My first Martin Luther King speech.
How great the word.

It was here
Under this very orange tree,
On this very peace of earth
That I first sang
With a hummingbird.
How great the song.

This orange tree knows me,
It is my friend,
I trust it and
It taste good.

IF YU SMELL

If yu smell a smell
Dat makes your nostrils swell,
Be thankful dat yu have a nose at all,
An if yu cannot tell
When your flowers are unwell,
Your nose may be a little bit too small.

IF YU TASTE

If yu taste your lips
Let me give yu a tip,
De bottom one tastes different from de top,
An if yu taste parsnips
Dat taste a bit like chips
I think yu should return dem to de shop.

IF YU TOUCH

If yu touch me front
I'll have to touch yu back,
An if yu touch me feet I will giggle,
Sometimes I may grunt
Like a touchy maniac
If yu touch me belly in de middle.

U.N. (UNITED NEIGHBOURS)

Me is a simple Jamaican man
From Jamaica in de Caribbean
Me look like an African
Because Africa is me Motherlan.

Me neighbour is a European
Born an bred in Engerlan
An we juss cannot understan
Why nations cannot live as wan.

KISS AND SMELL

So and so loved kissing flowers
Small ones and ones fully grown,
Sometimes they kissed them for hours
They could not leave them alone,
Their favourite places were gardens
Or big parks where big flowers grew,
They would go looking for plants then
Do all that kissing they do.

Flowers who knew of the duo
Knew it was very good fun,
Many would wait in a neat row
Waiting for when they would come,
People who saw them could not tell
What all this kissing stuff meant,
The doctors report said they seem well
And it's lawful to sniff with intent.

Spring times and summers were just great
Flowers would grow a big smile
Everything grew at a fast rate
When rains came to help out the soil,
Indoors they always kiss pot plants
And if they had any time spare,
They would wait on street corners for a chance
To kiss flowers in somebodies hair.

So and so loved kissing flowers
Any shape, colour or size
They said 'All flowers are ours'
And 'We are for flowers'
That's wise,
So and so keep kissing flowers
Some say they may have kissed fern,
And maybe I've gone a bit sour
Waiting so long for my turn.

NO REASON, NO RHYME

A smart poem called Limerick
Waz trying to rhyme very quick
She went berserk
When her rhyme didn't work
And now she is quite
Unwell.

HEALTH CARE

All yu Presidents
Think of de residents,
Queens an Kings
Start sharing,
City planners
Hav sum manners,
Prime ministers please
Think of de trees.

Those dat sail
Tek care of de whales,
De strong should seek
To strengthen de weak,
Lovers of art
Should play their part,
An all those upon it
Tek care of de planet.

ALL YOU SEA

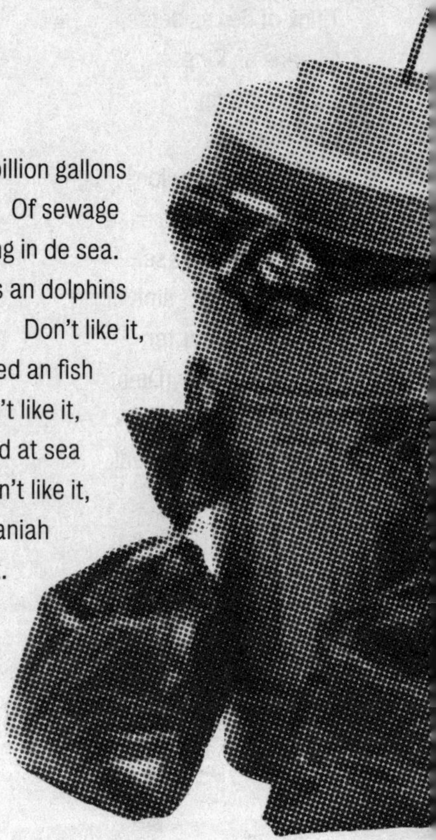

Three billion gallons
Of sewage
Floating in de sea.
Whales an dolphins
Don't like it,
Seaweed an fish
Don't like it,
De dead at sea
Don't like it,
Zephaniah
Don't like it.

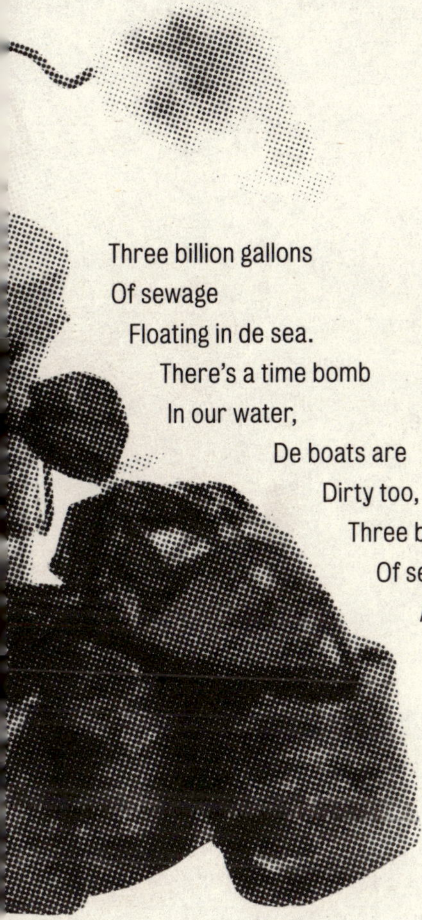

Three billion gallons
Of sewage
Floating in de sea.
There's a time bomb
In our water,
De boats are
Dirty too,
Three billion gallons
Of sewage,
All for you.

DOWN TO EARTH

You gotta be cool
To live on the sun
It's pure central heating up there,
With no swimming pool
You'll bake like a bun
And fire will burn off your hair.

There are no cars
Or bikes upon Mars
And there is still nothing to breathe,
There's no superstars
Playing guitars
And it is not easy to leave.

The moon is not **cheese**
The moon is not cake
I know it's a wonderful sight,
Up there if you sneeze
Or loud noises make
They'll simply get lost in the night.

Skywards I **stare**
To see what is there
Some say that I am wasting my time,
Well I must declare
I can't see no air
But I see a very good rhyme.

DEREK IN HEAVEN

Derek in heaven
Swallowed a poem
That little poem
Just kept on growing,
Derek grew bigger
Until she was big
Then Derek the beetle
Turned into a pig.
This pig could fly
Well that's what I heard
Then our heavenly piggy
Turned into a bird,
Bird brainy Derek
Loved flying around
In this animal heaven
Where poems are found.
What's more amazing
Is that in her youth
Bird brainy Derek
Turned into a fruit,
Derek got ripe
Derek stood proud
And this juicy fruity
Would shout very loud,
This musical fruit
Had a wonderful habit
Of rapping

So then she turned into a rabbit,
One day she went into
God's great big hat
And what did she do,
She turned into a rat.
This cool rat rapper
Had the eyes of an eagle
One day as she rapped
She turned into a beetle,
Then Derek the beetle
Found heaven's big tree,
There she thrives on a diet
Of pure poetry.

GOOD HOPE

I believe
There is enough food
On this planet
For everyone.

I believe
That it is possible
For all people
To live in peace.

I believe
We can live
Without guns,
I believe everyone
Is important.

I believe there are good Christians
And good Muslims,
Good Jews
And good not sures,
I believe
There is good in everyone
I believe in people.

If I did not believe
I would stop writing.

I know
Every day
Children cry for water,
And every day
Racists attack,
Still every day
Children play
With no care for colour.

So I believe **there is hope**
And I hope
That there are many believers
Believing
There is hope,
That is what I hope
And this is what I believe,
I believe in you,
Believe me.

DANNY LIVES ON

Danny the cat
Died last week
Killed by kicks
Of human feet,
I am sorry to say
He passed away,
A houseful of tears
I cried that day.
Danny's not with me any more
Human beings beat him
I don't know what for,
I know that some animals
Kill others to eat
But this gang just wanted to
Fight on the streets.

Danny my friend
Waz walking home
Not making trouble
And all on his own,
A few neighbours told me
That Danny then ran
And a human being kick him
To prove he's a man,
But what kind of man
Could this wicked be

I think he's a coward
He couldn't fight me.
What kind of world do we live in today,
When our future adults
Treat life this way.

Dear **Reader**,
Excuse me,
I am hurting inside,
I just don't think that we
Are near civilized,
We know how to fly
And we sail on the sea
But we don't understand
That life is a tree,
And Danny my friend
If this message gets through
You'll know this poet
Is thinking of you,
These animal beaters
Are so filled with hate,
Us animal lovers
Know Danny waz great.

SOMETHING TO WORRY ABOUT

Nothing rhymes wid **nothing**
I discovered dat today
Now I hav two more words
To help me rhyme away,

Nothing + nothing = (**nothing**)

I am good at maths as well
I feel like a professor
As me head begins to swell.

If I start wid **nothing**
I hav **nothing** to lose
And now dat I hav two **nothings**
It's easier to choose,
Nothing gets me worried
I hope you overstand
I am now enjoying **nothing**
And I hav **nothing** planned.

I am busy doing **nothing**
Me parents think it's great
I am in luv wid **nothing**
And there's **nothing** dat I hate,
I will give you **nothing**
So you hav **nothing** to fear
Let me tell you **nothing**
I hav **nothing** to declare.

Nothing's rong wid **nothing**
It's such a great idea
It need not be created
I hav **nothing** to share,
Nothing rhymes wid **nothing**
There waz **nothing** at de start
And I can't give you anything
When there's

nothing

in my heart.

GOING LOTTO

I think I've won the lottery
My goodness me I am rich
Now I'll throw away my clothes
And replace every stitch,
I think I've won the lottery
I am going to buy some fame
I am going to buy my own police
Who will protect my name.

I am going to take some money
And buy myself a plane
And when I've been around the world
I'll just go round again,
I am going to take some money
And buy some quietness
I am going to buy a doctor
Who can get rid of my stress.

I am going to buy me every zoo
And let the animals out
Then I'll get my quietness
And really, really shout,
I'll do just what I want to
With all that money of mine
And if I get too busy
I'll buy myself some time.

I think I've won the lottery

I think, I think, I think
I think
Therefore
I think I'll buy myself
The missing link,
And if I've won the lottery
I'll buy lots of goodbyes
Then I will give them happily
To all the racist guys.

I think I've won the lottery

My goodness greatness me
I must get some security
And protect my prize money,
But don't go telling everybody
Think before you speak
I get this feeling regularly
I thought the same last week.

FAIR DEAL

Rick de rapper
Met a shopper
At de May Day fair,
Said Rick de rapper
To de shopper,
'What are you doing here?'
De shopper said,
'I come to buy a Helter Skelter Rick,
I've got a bit of money
And I've got to spend it quick!'

Rick de rapper said,
'Look shopper,
Let's be sensible,
You cannot buy that Helter Skelter
It's unbuyable.'
De shopper started crying
He was a saddened chap,
But it was not for buying
Rick de rapper
Told him dat.

They met one hour later,
By the First Aid shelter,
De shopper told de rapper
Dat he owns de Helter Skelter,
Rick said,
'I am sure you can't buy
Helter Skelters here.'
De shopper said,
'Us millionaires
Just simply buy the fair.'

WALKING BLACK HOME

That day waz
A bad day,

I walked for
Many miles,

Unlike me,
I did not

Return any
Smiles.

Tired,

Weak
And
Hungry,

But I
Would not
Turn

Back,

Sometimes it's hard
To get a taxi
When you're **Black.**

PROTEST POETS

Dem sey
Dere is now
A computer
Dat writes poems,
Or to put it another way,
A computer
Dat's a poet.

How does it relax?
Wot's its inspiration?
An does it sign autographs?
Does it wake up
In de middle of de night
An sey,
'I've got a great idea,
Where's me floppy disk?'
Or is it one of those poets
Dat don't say much.

Does it try to get its friends writing?
Does it travel on de Internet?
How does it tek criticism?
If computers hav to be programmed
Is a computer poet programmed by poets or mechanics?
How does such a poet perform poems,
An do dey perform to people
Or computers?

Is dere a factory somewhere
Full of poets in white coats
Wid screwdrivers an microchips in their pockets?

These are de questions
Dat every decent human poet should ask,
We human poets should unite
Lest we pass on to future poets
A world in which
Poets do not fall in love
Or mek mistakes
An all inspiration is programmed,

WE DEMAND A FUTURE
Where poets do silly things,
Like
Sleep in socks,
Wear flares,
An talk to caterpillars,
A future where poets
Scratch,
Wonder,
An cry on de page.

DOUBLE TALK

Not, not, not, not
A lot, a lot, a lot, a lot
Of, of, of, of
People, people, people, people
Know, know, know, know
Dat, dat, dat, dat
Dis, dis, dis, dis
Page, page, page, page
Has, has, has, has
A great, a great, a great, a great
Echo, echo, echo, echo, echo, echo, echo,
echo, echo, echo.

, a lot

e, people, people

know, know

dat

dis

, page, page

has, has

great, a great, a great

echo, echo, ec

FOOTBALL MAD

Oh no, bless my soul
Clever Trevor's scored a goal.

So he runs up the pitch
And wriggles his botty,
He is kissed by ten men
All sweaty and snotty,
Now he's waving his fist
To the Queen who just stares
The lad's going crazy
But everyone cheers.
Now what's he doing?
He's chewing the cud!
Now what's he doing?
He's rolling in mud!
Now he is crying
I think he's in pain
Now what's he doing?
He's smiling again.

On no, bless my soul
Clever Trevor's scored a goal.

He's doing gymnastics
He's doing some mime
He's kissing the ground
For a very long time,
He's now on his back
With his feet in the air
Now he's gone all religious
And stopped for a prayer.
Did he pray for the sick?
Did he pray for the poor?
No, he prayed for the ball
And he prayed to score.
No one but no one
Can re-start the game
Until Trevor has had
His moment of fame.

Oh no, bless my soul
Clever Trevor's scored a goal,
He kicked the ball into the net
How much money will he get?

BIG BABY

Once I was a twinkle
In my father's eye,
Once I was my mother's
Dream come true,
Now I am a hippy
Rappy Rasta guy
Trying to invent
A rhyme or two.

Once I was a
Smelly little baby,
Once I was kissed
Every single day,
Now everybody thinks
That I am crazy
As I dilly dally dolly
On my way.

HOME ALONE

Mum's got a telly of her own
Dad's got a telly of his own
Baby got a telly of his own
Little sister got a telly of her own.

Cat got a telly of her own
Mouse got a telly of his own
I got a telly of my own
To make me feel at home.

HIP-HOP COP

He looks a bit like
Fred Astaire
He's off on tour
Everywhere,
He can't stop
He luvs to rock,
He's de hip-hop cop
From de big cop shop.

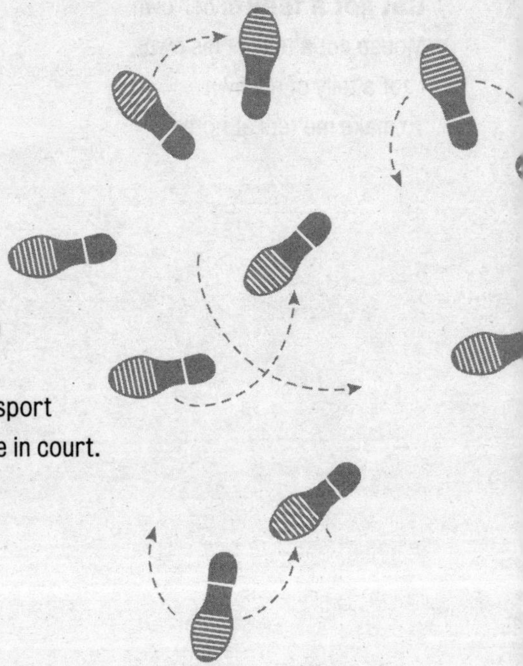

Dressed in blue
He funky chickens
He danced right through
Me vegan kitchen,
Dancing is his favourite sport
I've even seen him dance in court.

He's de hip-hop cop
From de big cop shop,
Always there
An liked a lot,
Me mom thinks he's really sweet
He is always on
De beat,

He's de hip-hop cop
From de big cop shop,
A criminal
He never got,
But he got riddim
He got soul
An he is
Fifty-five years old.

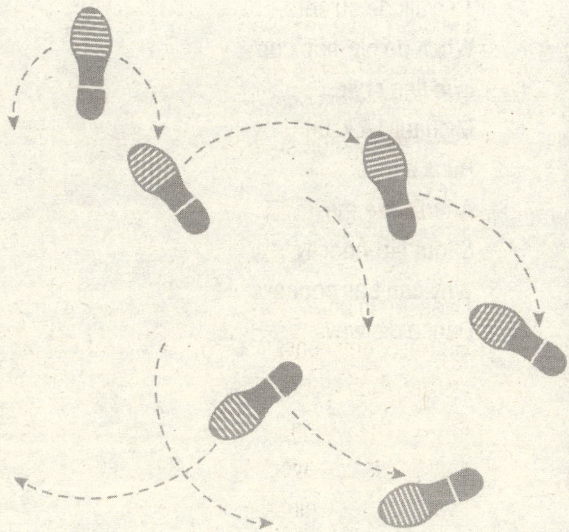

He raps in his
Walkie talkie
To a copper
In Milwaukee,
Once he caught
Discomania
On a dance floor
In Romania,
Now de hip-hop cop
Is doing fine
His body's always
Doing time,
Never keen to
Make arrest
But always keen
To dance his best.

When de hip-hop cop
Is in our town
There is no crime
We all get down,
To de wicked beat
Wid our wicked feet
An it's very safe
To walk de streets,
When de hip-hop cop
Is in fine style
Michael Jackson
Runs a mile
An folk like me
Shout hip-hooray,
Why can't all coppers
Dance dis way.

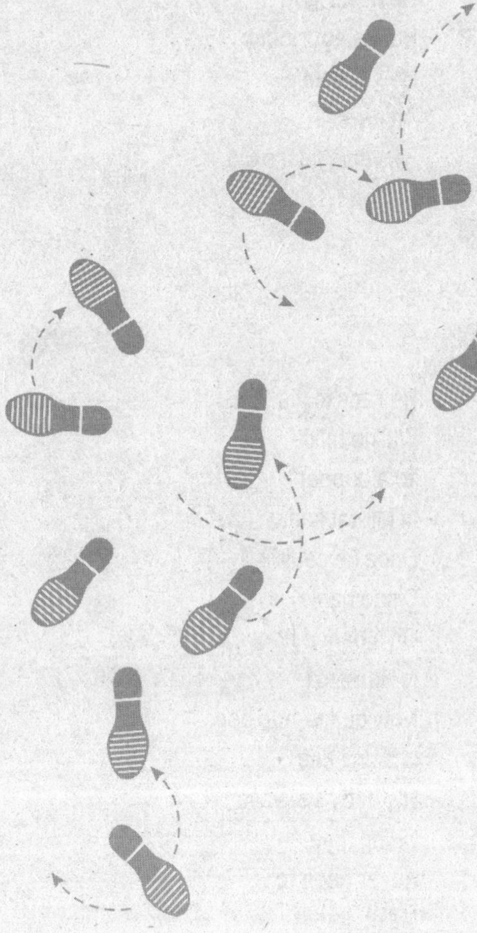

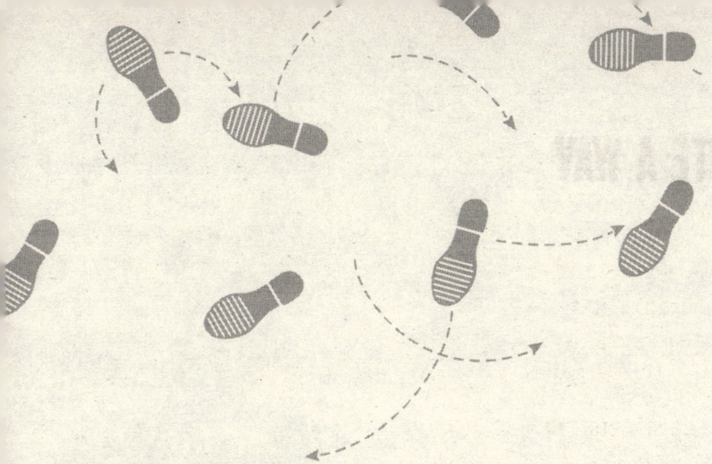

He's de hip-hop cop
From de big cop shop
Always there
An liked a lot
He lays down
De groovy law
An he
Really
Knows de score,
He's de hip-hop cop
From de big cop shop
He seems to dance
Wid ease
Non-stop,
No one's ever seen
Him stumble,
In dis urban
Concrete jungle.

WRITE A WAY

Kitty's poem flew like a kite

Benny wrote a poem dat bends,

Annie wrote a poem dat ascends

And **Penny** wrote a poem dat writes.

PENCIL ME IN

I know a pencil
Full of lead,
It knows the thoughts
Within my head,
It knows my secrets
And my fears,
It draws a line
Right through my tears.
I know a pencil
Old and grey,
Willing to work
Both night and day,
Fat and lovely
Light and fine,
It moves with me
Through space and time.

Be they good
Or be they bad,
It tells of all
The dreams I have,
And when I have
No oar to row,
It writes a way
And lets me go.
When baby words
Are crying loud,
It touches words

And makes me proud,
A work of art
It is no fake,
It really has
A point to make.

This pencil sees
The best of me,
The worst
And all the rest
Of me,
And as I go
Through puberty,
It changes all my
Poetry.
It goes with me
On all my tours,
It fought with me
In all word wars,
And peacefully
This pencil tries
To help me learn
And make me wise.

Every pencil needs a hand
And every mind needs to expand,
I know a pencil,
What you see
Is me and it
In harmony.

FUNKY CHICKEN

A funky chicken ate my corn
But really I don't mind,
My funky friend eats my dinner
Every time I dine,
He said that he's a big fan
Of my rhyming poetry,
So when we get together
We double talk turkey.

A funky chicken nicked my pants
But I think that's OK,
I'm the kind of rhymer
That wears two pairs anyway,
Yesterday he nicked my lemon flavoured socks,
And the last time that I saw him
He was growing dreadlocks.

A funky chicken nicked my rhyme
And I was lost for words,
So I went and made some poems,
With the bees and the birds,
He can have some more rhymes
If he gives me a chance,
To tune in then chicken out
And learn his funky dance.

A funky chicken spent my cash
I'm broke but I don't care,
This chicken has so much style
The chicks just stand and stare,
Human beings are unaware
Of all the fun they're missing,
Until they see this very funky chicken
Funky Chicken.

This feathery funky flapper
Is really flipping great,
He's the pick of the pops with the pecker
And I'm proud that he's my mate,
When he nicked my music
I told him not to stop,
One day I'll introduce him to
That friendly hip-hop cop.

WICKED
WORLD

HONGI

They don't mind shaking hands
But you have to understand,
That a really friendly Maori
Wants to Hongi.

It may all seem quite grand
And you may have other plans,
But a really friendly Maori
Wants to Hongi.

After you have exchanged names
It is obviously plain,
That a really friendly Maori
Wants to Hongi.

If you plan to play some games
The house rules are just the same,
You see every friendly Maori
Wants to Hongi.

In New Zealand no one stares
They've been doing it for years,
They know that a really friendly Maori
Wants to Hongi.

Usually it's done in pairs
And it shows how much they care,
So a really friendly Maori
Wants to Hongi.

When the game is lost and won
Even in the midday sun,
Even then a friendly Maori
Wants to Hongi.

It's the way greetings are done
And they can be real good fun,
Yes a really friendly Maori
Wants to Hongi.

If you've just arrived from Belgium
And you have friends in New Zealand,
You should know that friendly Maoris
Want to Hongi.

It don't matter where you come from
It's a most respectful welcome,
You see every friendly Maori
Wants to Hongi.

If you are feeling low
They have ways to make you glow,
Cheer up, every friendly Maori
Wants to Hongi.

They're originals you know
That is why I want to go,
Because every friendly Maori
Wants to Hongi.

BEFORE ALL THESE CITIES

We brave Apache once lived on the plains
Under the hot sun where it hardly rains,
We fought all who came to steal our territory
That is why we are called the brave Apache.

When we did the snake dance we felt like a **snake**
Not scared of anything and very awake,
We can move as quick as the blink of an eye
We never give up without giving a try.

We wake in the morning and offer a prayer
That says we are thankful for all that is here,
We're thankful for rain, light and big buffalo
We're thankful for movement wherever we go.

Once we were masters of self-education
Now we all live on a dry reservation,
Before all these cities, and factories and trains
We brave Apache once lived on the plains.

THE CELTS

They lived in France and Germany
The Celts
They lived in France and Germany
The Celts
They spread their community
Through Holland, Spain and Italy
They left their mark on history
The Celts.

They moved around for centuries
The Celts
They moved around for centuries
The Celts
They moved on land, they moved on sea
From Africa to Brittany
They had great fun in Anglesey
The Celts.

They worked with silver, bronze and gold
The Celts
They worked with silver, bronze and gold
The Celts
The goods they made were bought and sold
Then thrown away when they got old
And they made lucky charms to hold
The Celts.

They were very agricultural
The Celts
They were very agricultural
The Celts
They were functional and pastoral
And really quite exceptional
And they were three-dimensional
The Celts.

They had a great big empire
The Celts
They had a great big empire
The Celts
But just like every empire
For sure it had to expire
They even reigned in Hertfordshire
The Celts.

They never had an emperor
The Celts
They never had an emperor
The Celts
They made homes in Macedonia
Turkey and Transylvania
But they never had an emperor
The Celts.

They loved their oral poetry
The Celts
They loved their oral poetry
The Celts
A great night in for them you see
Was listening to a good story
They really used their memory
The Celts.

They have languages that still survive
The Celts
They have languages that still survive
The Celts
They are a tough and sturdy tribe
In Wales and Scotland they survive
And in Ireland they really thrive
The Celts.

A MYSTERY FROM HISTORY

Who built that pyramid?
Waz it Joe or waz it Sid?
Waz it Meena or Javid?
Where they old, waz it a kid?

Who built that pyramid?
Waz it Rachel or David?
Waz it built slow or rapid?
Where they well dressed or naked?

Who built that pyramid?
Waz it Johnny or Alfred?
Waz it Assad or Syed?
It's amazing wot they did.

Who built that pyramid?
It's great that they succeeded
Where they single or married?
And who did they build it wid?

VERY MONGOLIAN

The people of Mongolia
Are very, very few,
I went to North Mongolia
And I met one or two,
When I went to the southern parts
I met three, four, or five,
I travelled west on a big brown horse
With built-in overdrive.

When chilly winds went up my nose
I couldn't help but sneeze,
And I couldn't help but notice
That there wasn't any trees,
The mountain and the hillsides there
Were lovely to behold
But I couldn't help but notice
That it was very, very cold.

The people of Mongolia
Are very, very strong,
You have to be when it's that cold
If you want to last for long,
Still, once a year things change
They do have summers there you know,
But you must be quick to see them,
Easy come and easy go.

In Mongolia they have circular homes
That are made of dark timber,
This type of house is moveable
It's what's known as a ger,
And at the centre of the ger
A hole will let in light,
But when I tried to build one
I just couldn't get it right.

Most people in Mongolia
Will own a big warm coat,
And many wise Mongolians
Are humans, sheep and goats,
Mongolia's the kind of place
Where everyone is cool,
And the things that animals leave behind
Are used each day as fuel.

The people of Mongolia
Are very, very few,
I went to East Mongolia
And met another two,
To tell the truth I met much more
Than five or six or seven,
Mongolia's a very, very, very
Cold heaven.

WHOSLAND

At dawn one morn
After eight weeks of sailing,
The Europeans landed
On the gold, sandy beach.

After praying
They made their way
Inland,
With their flags in their hands
And an empire on their minds.

Soon they came across a small village,
All the people came out to see them,
The villagers thought they had come with great knowledge
And wisdom from afar.
Having never seen Europeans before
This was new and exciting.

When the captain of the ship
Met the elder of the village
He still had a flag in his hand
And an empire on his mind.

'What did you call this land before
we arrived?'
said the captain.

'Ours'
said the village elder,

'Ours.'

HIM IN THE HIMALAYAS

He's quiet
He's careful
He's not a millionaire
He never ever swears,
Him in the Himalayas.

He smiles
When
He means it
And not because you're there,
He loves you and he cares,
Him in the Himalayas.

His home is
So simple,
He's happy living there
He's happy he declares,
Him in the Himalayas.

He's quite close
To nature,
They say he talks to bears
And respects what is theirs,
Him in the Himalayas.

His robe
Is bright orange
And he don't need no hair,
He doesn't have
nightmares,
Him in the Himalayas.

He loves rain
He loves sun
Snow causes no despair,
He does his own repairs,
Him in the Himalayas.

Have no doubt
He's way out
He lives where most won't dare
With very little fears,
Him in the Himalayas.

He breathes deep
The freshest air,
He's very much aware,
He's always saying prayers,
Him in the Himalayas.

IN INDONESIA

In Indonesia
There are Moslems and Hindus
In Indonesia
There are Buddhists and Sikhs
In Indonesia
There's more than three hundred tribal groups
Using just as many different ways to speak.

In Indonesia
There's a tribe that's called the Javanese
And another one that's called the Sundanese,
People famous for their batiks are called Balinese
Not to be confused with others known as Madurese.

There are Makasarese, Ambonese and Chinese
There are Torajas and Dayaks and Papuans
And they all live on all these little islands
Eating long grain rice and voicing their opinions.

In Indonesia
Wayang Topeng is masked dance,
And the people are proud of the masks they make,
If you want to go somewhere that's really boring
And you go there
Then you're making a mistake.

In Indonesia
There's shadow plays called Wayang Kulit
And a puppet play is called a Wanyang Golek,
So if you want to find some Indonesian culture
You'll have to learn some new words or
Simply forget it.

FEARLESS BUSHMEN

The bushmen of the Kalahari desert
Painted themselves on rocks
With wildebeests and giraffes
Thousands of years ago.
And still today they say
To boast is sinful
Arrogance is evil.
And although some say today that they
Are the earliest hunter-gatherers known
They never hunt for sport
They think that's rude,
They hunt for food.

They earn respect by sharing
Being true to their word
And caring.
They refuse to own land but
They can build a house in two days
And take it down in four hours.

Three generations will live together.
A girl will grow up to feed her mother
Who feeds the mother
That once fed her.
To get that food a girl will walk
Upon the hot desert sands
An average of a thousand miles a year.

Their footprints are uniquely small
For people who travel so much
To find melons or mongongo trees,
And those small dark and nimble feet
May spend two days chasing a deer.
Charity, respect and tolerance
Are watchwords for these ancient folk
Who spend their evenings singing songs
Around their campfires.

These hunter-gatherers are fearless
But peaceful,
They will never argue with a mamba snake,
When one is seen heading towards the village
They kiss the Earth
And move the village.

GLORIOUS LOSERS

They were mighty warriors
They feared no living thing,
They broke down all barriers
When they were conquering,
Nearly all their enemies
Had to up and run,
When those guys got military
It seems they always won.

When they found a city
They took all that they saw,
They did not have no pity
When they were out at war,
When they met new neighbours
Over the garden wall,
They cut them up with razors
Then enslaved or killed them all.

They battled on the playing fields
They battled in the valley,
They battled with their spears and shields
And even in the alleys,
They would not leave the battleground
Without feeling glorious,
So when some foreign tribes were found
They had to be victorious.

But every now and then it's said
The tables must be turned
And someone may just lose their head
If lessons are not learnt,
These fighters would not tell their foe
They always needed light,
You see the Aztecs of Old Mexico
Just would not fight at night.

When they woke up in the morning
They fought to get some food,
If things were getting boring
They would fight to change the mood,
The men fought over women
And the women fought for men,
When they saw people swimming
They dived in and fought with them.

Throughout Central America
The Aztecs caused such fear,
If you were unfamiliar
They'd make you disappear,
For reasons that we still don't know
(They weren't being polite),
You see the Aztecs of Old Mexico
Just would not fight at night.

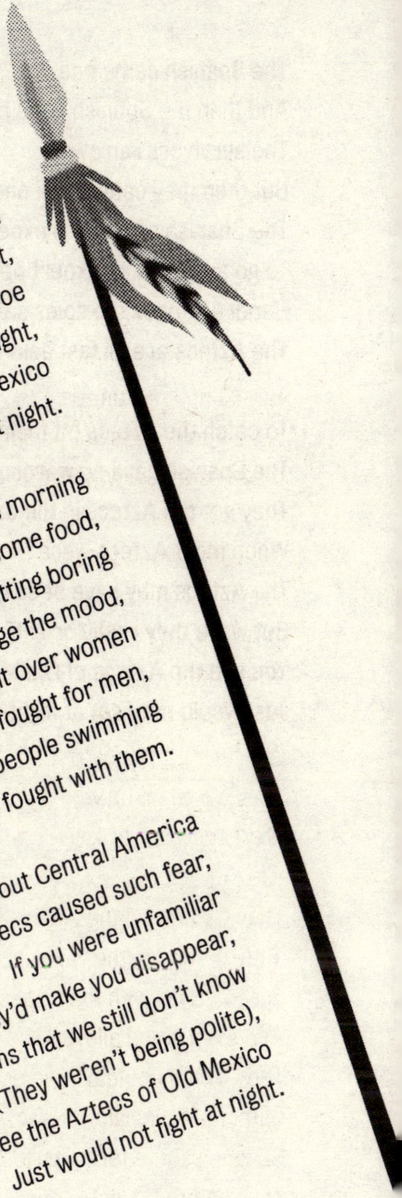

The Spanish came one day
And then the Spanish got a beating,
The survivors ran away
But then they came back one fine evening,
The Spanish sent some expert spies
To go and have an expert peep,
Reporting back the spies said, 'Guys,
The Aztecs are all fast asleep!'

To catch the Aztecs off their mark
The Spanish gave no warning,
They got the Aztecs in the dark
When most Aztecs were snoring,
The Aztecs may have been macho
But were they really bright?
You see the Aztecs of Old Mexico
Just would not fight at night.

WAITING FOR ADU

I lost my friend called Adu
I haven't seen him for some time
And I was really worried
He was a great friend of mine.

Adu my friend has gone and
I really miss that kid,
I really miss the funny things
That my mate Adu did.

The last time that I saw him
He was cracking wicked jokes,
We were exchanging stories
Underneath a giant oak.

When I was last with Adu
We were having a great time
Eating nuts and berries
And rapping wicked rhymes.

One day I went to visit him but
His village was not there
And I couldn't see his family
Or his neighbours anywhere.

I shouted out loud, 'Adu,
Hey Adu, where are you?'
The reply was stony silence
And my heart was feeling blue.

I turned to face my village
Then I ran quickly home,
I asked my Mommy why she thought
He left me all alone.

She said, 'Dear son, don't worry and
There's no need to feel sad
That is just his way of life
Adu is a nomad.'

I said, 'What's a nomad, Mommy?'
As I screwed up my face,
She explained to me that nomads
Move around from place to place.

That night when I stopped crying
And I realized it was true,
My Mommy sat and told me of
The things that nomads do.

Some nomads move for food
Some move for the weather
Some move in small family groups
Some large groups move together.

They do not value property
The family must have honour
Most of them do not use money
They just value each other.

Most countries have some nomads
Some people put them down
But since the beginning of time
They have always moved around.

Now I'm not crying for Adu
His going made me learn
Because he is a nomad
One day Adu may return.

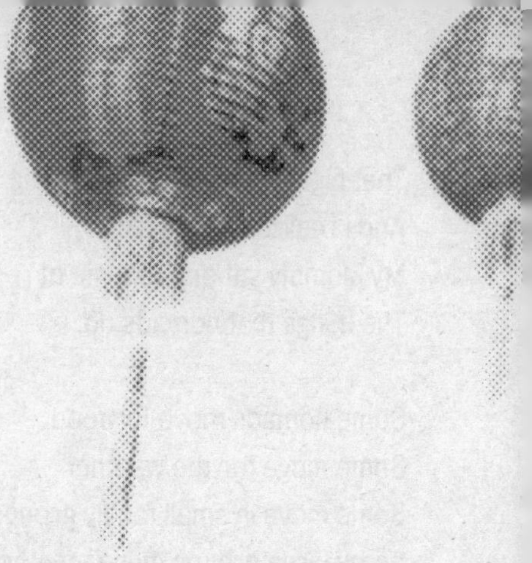

THINK CHINESE

Did you know that
China has more people
Than anywhere?

China has more mouths to feed
China has more homes,
China has more books to read,
More heads, more hair, more combs,
China has more people
Than anywhere I've known,
So the Chinese have to make sure
That lots of food is grown.
China has more people
Than anywhere,
And in China it's hard to be alone.

China has more people
Than anywhere.

In China there's more trousers
In China there's more boys,
In China there's more girls
And in China there's more toys,
In China there's more kisses,
Or that's what I've been told,
I really think that this is
A country to behold.

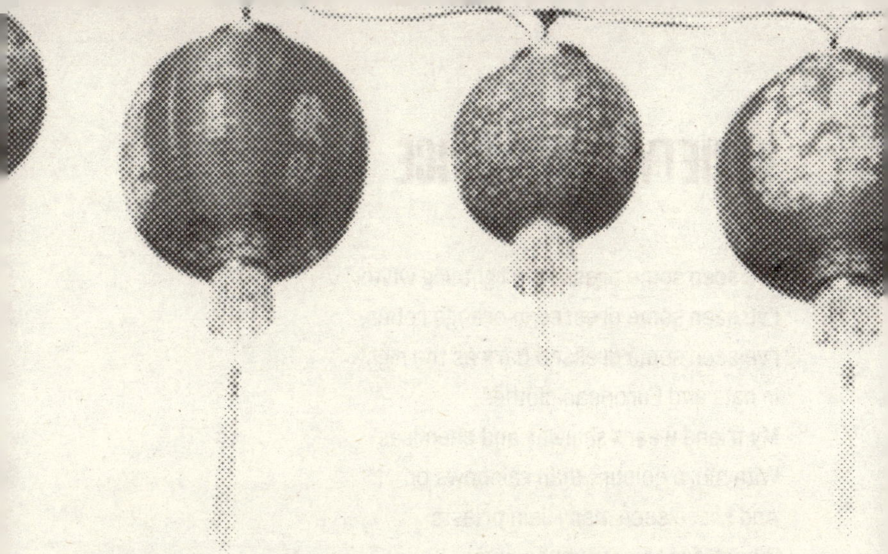

China has more people
Than anywhere,
And most of the people live
To be quite old.

China has more people
Than anywhere.

You should not forget
That China has some wicked verse,
The Chinese alphabet
Is the biggest in the universe,
If all the people in China clapped
The Earth would really shake,
And if all the people in China rapped
Sweet music they would make.
China has more people
Than anywhere,
And that's just one reason why China is great.

VARIETY IS THE SPICE

I've seen some dressed in lightning white
I've seen some dressed in orange robes,
I've seen some dressed dark as the night
In hats and European clothes,
My friend wears shalwar and chemises
With more colours than rainbows on
And I have seen many Jain priests
Who dress to not hurt anyone.

Millions travel upon their bikes
And millions travel in their cars
And millions dream of being like
Those super Bollywood film stars,
They dance Hindi, Hip-hop and Jazz
So people don't believe the hype,
Because there is no such thing as
An average Indian stereotype.

They are so rich, they are so poor
And millions are so in-between
Some want for nothing, some want more
And some are quick and very keen,
Some of them wear their hair so short
Some of the girls wear flowered frocks,
In this nation of many sorts
You'll find Sadhus with long dreadlocks.

Some of them live in villages
Some of them live in high-rise flats,
Some of them have big businesses
Some just do bits of this and that,
Sometimes I know that I've been wrong
But now I know that I am right,
Because I know that there's no one
Average Indian stereotype.

Many are wise, many are smart
Many just simply want to be,
Many are light, many are dark
And many of them are just like me,
Many live on cold mountain tops
Many live in the heat below,
Many have no spare time to stop
Many have no spare time to go.

Some of them pray, some of them don't
Some of them sing, some of them won't,
Some of them serve, some of them cook
Some like to read rhymes in a book,
I may not be smart, wise and great
But this time I know I am right,
Make sure that you make no mistake
There is no Indian stereotype.

THE POLE WITH NO SOUL

I'm wondering
How does he do it?
I'm wondering
What is his role?
I'm speaking of my friend Nobody
Nobody lives by the South Pole.

He ain't got no good friends
To talk to
He ain't got nobody to kiss,
There isn't much there
That he can do,
He can't go on living
Like this.

He ain't got no brothers
Or sisters
He ain't got no one
At his side
There's no Mrs
And there's no Mr's
He has no language,
He's from no tribe.

It's so strange to be
With no history
It's so strange that
Nobody's there

I wonder
What his future will be
But Nobody don't seem to care.

Nobody's dancing
He's not on the phone,
There is no music
And he's all alone,
Nobody's eating
Nobody's sharing
Nobody's reading
And Nobody's hearing,
Nobody's not having
The time of his life,
Nobody's talking to
No one from Fife,
Nobody's talking
And saying nothing,
Nobody's a poet
And nobody's singing.

I'm wondering
How does he do it?
It must take
So much self-control,
I'm speaking of my friend Nobody
Nobody lives by the South Pole.

THE POLE WITH NO POLES

The North Pole
Is not fit for humans,

You won't find a house
Or a tree,

You won't find Poles,
Germans, Or Cubans,

The North Pole is right in the sea.

EVERYONE'S FRIEND

My grandad said he was his friend
My grandma said she made him tea,
In Jamaica it seems to me
All grandparents knew Bob Marley.

My cousin said he built his house
My uncle put his carpet down,
My soccer-loving brother Paul
Claims that he kicked Bob Marley's ball.

My teacher said she taught him maths
Some joker said he taught him laughs,
The art school that is understaffed
Still claim they taught him arts and crafts.

My paperboy too has his views,
Said he knows secrets I could use,
When on a Caribbean cruise
He said he brought Bob Marley news.

A playwright in Montego Bay
Said Bob Marley was in her play,
But I could see right from the start
That really he was in her heart.

Rudie said he knew him well
He said he taught him ice hockey,

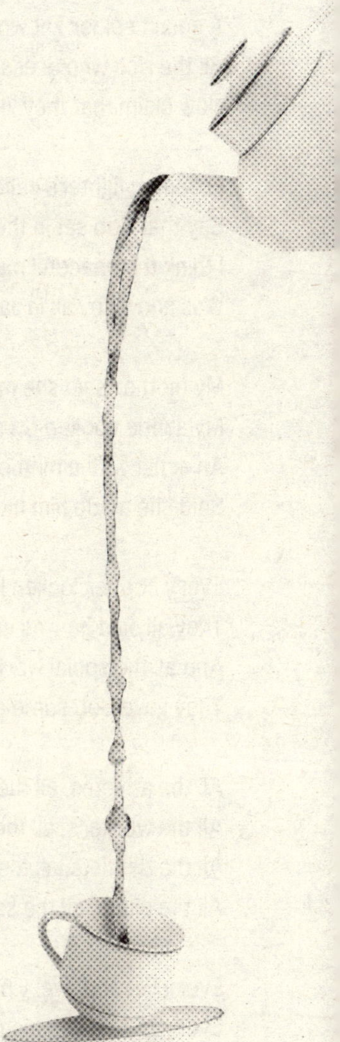

In Jamaica it seems to me
That all Rudies knew Bob Marley.

The coconut vendors, the pretenders
A smart spider known as Anansi
All the rich who dress up fancy
Now claim that they knew Bob Marley.

Freedom fighters called Maroons
Say that Bob sat in their rooms,
I think the peaceful music maker
Was known by all in Jamaica.

My mother said she made his hats
My auntie cooked his suppers,
An artist with a memory lapse
Said she made him nice bedcovers.

Every copper locked him up
They all said he was nice,
And all the social workers said
They gave Bob some advice.

All the athletes, all the drivers
All the workers, all the skivers,
All the dentists, all the tailors
All the pilots, all the sailors.

Every vet and every baker
Everybody in Jamaica,
Knew the brother personally
Everyone knew Bob Marley.

WE ARE THE CHEROKEE

We made sacred fires
As instructed
By our ancestors.

We farmed beans
And corn
In harmony
With our surroundings,
We knew the sun well.

We learnt to count
Each drop of rain,
And when we had their number
We thanked the sky
For each drop of rain.

We were so in love
That each one of us
Gave ourselves
And married the Earth.

We are the Cherokee.

Then there came a time
When the land beneath us
Was taken from us.
Even those of us who were not born then
Remember that time.

It was a time of great sadness,
The time of countless tears.

In the state now known as Texas
In the land now known as America
We taught ourselves
To avoid evil thoughts,
And welcome strangers.

Soon after welcoming the strangers
We found we had no land
To welcome strangers.
We learnt the language of the strangers
And tried talk,
Using the language of survival
We tried food,
Then in a desperate bid to save ourselves
We tried self-defence.

Now we live on the land
That we farmed and loved,
On this same piece of land
In a foreign country.

We are the Cherokee.

We can make for you
Beautiful baskets
To carry your dreams.

We can speak to you
In a language
That is older than the country
That contains us.

We can sing you songs
That were taught to us by big buffalo
And running bears,
To music that we gather
From the wind.

The cowboys were not that good
And we were not that bad.
All we wanted was
Our ways
Our names
Ourselves
And peace.

We are the Cherokee.

BENGALI RAP

My friends are very cool
My friends are very wise
Everyone is a winner
Everyone is a prize,
From the city of Dhaka
To the tracts of Chittagong,
My friends are very cool
Like a sweet rap song.

Some live in the city
Some live on the farm
They like to stay cool
They like to stay calm,
They say peace and love to all
Everywhere they go,
If they can say yes
They will never say no.

My friends from Bangladesh
My friends from Bangladesh
They're cool and they're fresh
My friends from Bangladesh.

Sometimes when I have time
I give my friends a call,
And then we all go sailing
In the Bay of Bengal,

That's what you can do
If your friends live by the sea
And if your friends are happy
To play in unity.

Sometimes my good friends
Will come and check me out
And then we get together
To rap, sing and shout,
And then when we get hungry
And we want something nice
We will cook and eat
Some tarka dall and rice.

My friends from Bangladesh
My friends from Bangladesh
They're cool and they're fresh
My friends from Bangladesh.

My friends have got me rocking
Each one is a star
Each one is a lover
And proud of who they are,
I know when they're thinking
That they're thinking of me
And of all the fun we have
With our rap poetry.

And when things get heavy
In the season of monsoons,
We all get together

To shelter in safe rooms,
I hope you get the message
It's loud and it's clear
My good friends are really cool
And they really do care.

My friends from Bangladesh
My friends from Bangladesh
They're cool and they're fresh
My friends from Bangladesh.

THE BRITISH

Serves over 60 million

Take some Picts, Celts and Silures
And let them settle,
Then overrun them with Roman conquerors.

Remove the Romans after approximately four hundred years
Add lots of Norman French to some
Angles, Saxons, Jutes and Vikings, then stir vigorously.

Mix some hot Chileans, cool Jamaicans, Dominicans,
Trinidadians and Bajans with some Ethiopians,
Chinese, Vietnamese and Sudanese.

Then take a blend of Somalians, Sri Lankans, Nigerians
And Pakistanis,
Combine with some Guyanese
And turn up the heat.

Sprinkle some fresh Indians, Malaysians, Bosnians,
Iraqis and Bangladeshis together with some
Afghans, Spanish, Turkish, Kurdish, Japanese
And Palestinians
Then add to the melting pot.

Leave the ingredients to simmer.

As they mix and blend allow their languages to flourish
Binding them together with English.

Allow time to be cool.

Add some unity, understanding and respect for the future
Serve with justice
And enjoy.

Note: All the ingredients are equally important.
Treating one ingredient better than another will
leave a bitter, unpleasant taste.
Warning: An unequal spread of justice will damage
the people and cause pain.

Give justice and equality to all.

A BIG WELCOME

Ladies and gentlemen
Boys and girls,
Put your hands together
And give a
BIG welcome
To the people from the
BIG forest
With the
BIG trees
Welcome
Please
The Pygmies.

Now as you see
The Pygmy is
BIG in Asia
BIG in Africa
And wherever they be
They specialize in living in
BIG harmony
With their neighbours.
So give them a
BIG round of applause,
They hate wars
Say a
BIG hello
To a
BIG hero
Ladies and gentlemen
Boys and girls,
The Pygmies.

KURDISH LAND

A question I keep asking is
Where is Kurdistan?
How come there is a nation
Of people with no land?
I keep asking the question,
It's so hard to understand,
Why some other people
Caused these people to disband.
More than twenty-two million Kurdish folk
Urgently need homes,
They don't want to live off charity,
Hand-outs, beg or live off loans,
It's a shame that all these people,
After all this time,
Have a language that's illegal,
So to speak the truth is a crime.

A question I keep asking is
Where is Kurdistan?
How come this great big nation
Is a nation
Without land?

ROMA PEOPLE ROAM

Since leaving northern India
Fifteen hundred years ago
They roamed all over Asia,
Europe and the Americas,
Over Australia and Africa,
The Roma people roam.

People began to call them gypsies,
They thought they came from Egypt
But they did not come from Egypt
Fifteen hundred years ago.
In fact they went all over
From North Africa to Dover
That's so natural for the Roma
The Roma people roam.

At times they have been hated
They have been separated
For not being related
To the people round about,
When things went wrong some blamed them
Without reason they shamed them,
When some folk couldn't tame them
What they did was throw them out.

It's said that some could read your future
Without knowing your past,
And they used to be famous
For all their arts and crafts,
It's said that this nomadic people
Have trod a million paths
Trading as they go
The Roma people roam.

These people have been everywhere
That human beings can go
Since leaving northern India
Fifteen hundred years ago,
So throughout the world you'll hear them
Singing in joyful tones,
And throughout the world you'll see them
Living in their homes,
People throughout the world will see them
Going straight through no-go zones,
Everywhere
The Roma people roam.

URDU POETS

Urdu poets speak wonders,
They are like magical wordsmiths,
They pluck words out of the sky
And create something for you to live for.

Urdu poets have a heavenly language
A language created by poets for poets,
A language that has turned a nation into poets,
Poets that love to speak to each other.

They bring glory to the bazaars
Hope to the pavements
Libraries to the mind,
They light up dark wordless days
Adding joy to eyes that are sad.
Urdu poets have been known to create paradise
In downtown Karachi
And wordplay on cricket fields,
Their verse so full of grace
Even when it is angry Urdu is beautiful.

Combine fire with water
Combine the calm with the storm,
Combine the greatest painters
With the greatest subjects
And you will have Urdu poets.

Knowledge can be tasty
To question can be delightful.

VOICES FOR CHOICES

If you did not have a car
You could still walk,
If you did not have a phone
You could still talk,
If you did not have a batter
Then the cricket would not matter
And you could still eat all your greens
Without a fork.

You could have a great big telly
With no vision,
We could all live without crime
And without prison,
Without dark we'd just have light
Without light we'd just have night
And if we tried we could eat cakes
That have not risen.

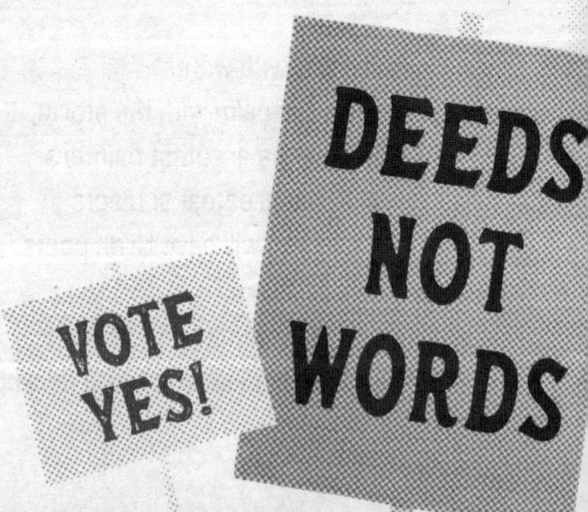

If we did not have cartoons
We'd all be funny,
And we'd probably be more equal
Without money,
We could live without computers
Dictators and persecutors
And our lives could still be quite sweet
Without honey.

But I'm trying to make sure
No one forgets,
That we really needed
Mighty Suffragettes,
If they did not raise their voices
Most of us would have no choices
And I think that we'd have many
Deep regrets.

INUIT

We live on top of the world.
From the icy deserts of Alaska
To the icy villages of Siberia
We are one,
We are at home.
Our lands are white and cold
American and European,
We are a close-knit
Far-flung tribe.
But we will not let distance
Or the weather
Hold us back,
If our snowmobiles struggle
And our motorboats freeze
Our dogs will take us quickly,
When electricity is low
And we have no gas to go
Our native dogs will rise up
And ride on.

There comes a time in every year
When many of us see no dusk,
The sun will shine for twenty-four hours one day
And then twenty-four hours the next day
Leaving no time for darkness
No hours for night.
This kind of sun is hot

Enough to warm our hearts
But it will not melt our future,
It lights the way
But it will not blind us,

This kind of sun
Reminds us of our place
On this planet.

Our name means people
Borders mean nothing
And the treatment of the fish we eat
Means everything to we who have no greens.
We can feel the past
We can carry the past with us but
We will not live in a frozen past
Unwilling to look beyond today,
Nor will we die in the fast lane
Of the super-modern highway.

In Greenland and Canada
We have roots,
We have relatives in tomorrow,
That is why as we look back
We look forward,
And as we look skywards
We look down.

Look up dear friends
And wave to us,
We live on top of the world.

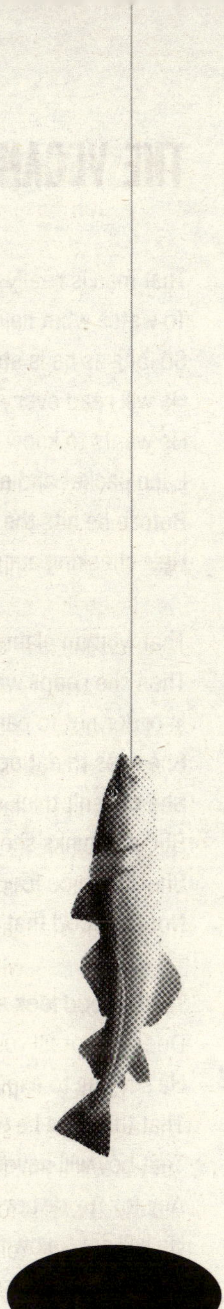

THE VEGANS

That man is really trying
To watch what he is buying,
So long as he is able
He will read every label,
He wants to know what's in
Each packet and each tin,
Before he hits the streets
He's checking out the eats.

That woman plants and grows
Then she reaps what she sows,
In order not to panic
She tries to eat organic,
She doesn't think she's perfect
But she thinks she's worth it,
She likes nice food that's memorable
Not bad food that's chemical.

Take a good look at that boy
Does he not fill you with joy?
He's trying to explain
That the thing he hates is pain,
That boy will never wear
Any fox fur or horsehair,
He will not follow fashion
His main thing is compassion.

That girl will not eat haddock
Or any animal product,
She's even learnt to think
About her bedtime drink,
She makes sure that her cuisine
Has the vitamins and protein
To keep her strong and healthy
Even if she is not wealthy.

All these people share
Concern for what they wear,
They check their shopping trolleys
And what goes in their bodies,
They are not all one colour
And it seems they live all over,
You see there are many reasons
Why these people are vegans.

WHO ARE WE?

So who are you?

Are you one of those
Tall people?
Are you one of those
Black people?
Or are you just one of
Those people,
Those other people,
You know
Them people?

We are calling us
Disabled people,
Able-bodied people,
Rich people,
Poor people,
Upper class people
Middle class people
Working class people
And even
Lower class people.

Who do we think we are?

We call some people
Foreign people,
Strange people,

Different people,
Why do we still
Label people?
Why do some people feel like
Chosen people?

OK
I know we come from different places,
We have different shades of skin,
And there are different ways of living
In the countries we live in,
And
Some people can do some things
And some people can do others,
But I think that we have to see
We're all sisters and brothers
And

Children may be small people
Adults may be big people
But when you get right down to it
All people are people,
And
As far as I can see
You're all related to me,
That is why I say that
All people are equal.

Now let your reply be true
Everybody
Who are you?

MY FRIEND MOUNTAIN FLOWER

She dresses in a thousand beads
    Each year she plants a thousand seeds.

With skill she weaves her wicker baskets
    She weaves her people's sleeping blankets.

She may not have what we call wealth
    But she can build her house herself.

Although she still lives with her Mom
    Experts can't work out where she's from.

She comes from a village people,
    They're famous for being peaceful.

If she gets married she won't roam
    Her husband must live in her home.

Some say that with the passing years
    Her way of life just disappears.

She's my friend, and you can quote me,
    Mountain Flower is a Hopi.

WE KNOW

Monkeys are not doing it,
Snakes are not doing it,
Neither are beetles or fleas,
Lizards are not doing it,
Birds are not doing it,
They know that we need the trees,
Mice are not doing it,
Lice are not doing it,
Cats are not doing it
Honest,
Bats are not doing it,
I know who's doing it,

Humans

are **killing**

the forest.

THE MAASAI GIRLS

The Maasai girls are dancing
And the earth is moving.

The Maasai girls are dancing
And there's thunder under feet.

The Maasai girls are dancing
And the mountains are alive,
Because the great dance of the tribe has just begun.

The Maasai girls are dancing
In Tanzania.

The Maasai girls dance beautiful
In Kenya.

The Maasai girls are dancing
And the boys are all amazed,
The Maasai girls are dancing in the sun.

A GRIOT WRITES

A Griot,
On the Streets,
In Villages,
Towns and Cities,
Senegal,
West Africa.

Dear People,

I hope that you are all well wherever you may be and that peace and love is in your lives.

Before coming to my main reason for writing to you, I would like to make it clear that we griots are not restricted to any one tribe, country or religion, and although we originate in the western parts of Africa, our offspring are taking our traditions to Europe, Australia and the American continent.

I have reason to believe that many of you around the world do not quite understand who we griots are and what we do. I have heard that your people-experts are a little confused by our role in our society.

A griot can be female or male, young or old. Many of us have been trained by our parents or the elders in our neighbourhoods and we will do our work for the rest of our lives. We are storytellers, it is our job to keep the ancient stories alive and sometimes we introduce new stories to deal with new subjects. We are poets, it is our job to keep the language alive by using wordplay and words that are beautiful and rhythmic. We are singers, we can play many instruments and sing many old and new songs for you. Some of our songs will be on traditional instruments and some of our griots use modern guitars and drums. You can be a griot and even sing Rock 'n' Roll, Soul, Reggae or Jazz, as long as it is done in the right spirit and with respect to the people. Many griots mix these styles with our local African music. We are historians, keeping alive memories from the past; we are prophets, looking forward into the future; we are dancers at weddings and other great ceremonies; we are actors on the stage of reality and we are newscasters. If our rulers are not being completely honest, or in areas where there are no newspapers and television, we are the ones who tell people what is really happening in the world.

So you see, people, we griots are many things, we are not just poets, or singers, dancers, or actors, we are all-round commentators, who work for the good of our community and not just for money. We are the oral tradition.

I really do hope this letter goes some way in helping you to understand exactly what a griot is, and how important our work is to us and our people.

By the way, we griots are comedians too. If I see you in Africa I'll tell you a joke that will make you laugh your chin off. But I don't want to talk about that now.

Say hello to your peace of the earth from me, and don't forget to kiss the sky.

Yours sincerely,

A Griot

IN THE MOUNTAINS OF TIBET

In the mountains of Tibet
It seems they won't forget
Their customs and their karma
And the Dalai Lama.
These non-violent monks and nuns
Fight for peace without big guns,
And non-violence makes them calmer,
As calm as the Dalai Lama.
As the farmer herds his yaks
The farmer knows the facts,
And that is why the farmer
Longs to see the Dalai Lama,
Yes it seems that in Tibet
Children simply won't forget
Their customs and their karma
And the Dalai Lama.

THE TOURISTS ARE COMING

Tell them to be careful
If they're not give them an earful
The tourists are coming
The tourists are coming.

They may want to party nightly
But tell them they must be tidy
The tourists are coming
The tourists are coming.

They must respect what we've planted
They should not take us for granted
The tourists are coming
The tourists are coming.

They should practise what they preach
When they're lying on our beach
The tourists are coming to play.

Because our land is sunny
They come here with their money
The tourists are coming
The tourists are coming.

We will not rant and rave
If they will behave
The tourists are coming
The tourists are coming.

We will not be bitter
If they don't drop their litter
The tourists are coming
The tourists are coming.

If they don't mess about
We will not kick them out
The tourists are coming to stay.

If by chance you see some
Try to make them welcome
The tourists are coming
The tourists are coming.

If they treat us good
They're welcome in the neighbourhood
The tourists are coming
The tourists are coming.

But if they're out of order
Show them to the border
The tourists are coming
The tourists are coming.

And if it does start raining
Tell them off if they're complaining
The tourists are coming I say.

Tell them that we love living
And money can't buy everything
The tourists are coming
The tourists are coming.

Call them names like fools and criminals
If they don't respect our animals
The tourists are coming
The tourists are coming.

Tell them if they can't keep the peace
That tourism may have to cease
The tourists are coming
The tourists are coming.

Tell them not to be greedy
And be careful where they wee wee
The tourists are coming this way.

PEOPLE NEED PEOPLE

To walk to
To talk to
To cry and rely on,
People will always need people.
To love and to miss
To hug and to kiss,
It's useful to have other people.
To whom will you moan
If you're all alone,
It's so hard to share
When no one is there,
There's not much to do
When there's no one but you,
People will always need people.

To please
To tease
To put you at ease,
People will always need people.
To make life appealing
And give life some meaning,
It's useful to have other people.
If you need a change
To whom will you turn,
If you need a lesson
From whom will you learn,
If you need to play

You'll know why I say
People will always need people.

As girlfriends
As boyfriends,
From Bombay
To Ostend,
People will always need people.
To have friendly fights with
And share tasty bites with,
It's useful to have other people.
People live in families
Gangs, posses and packs,
It seems we need company
Before we relax,
So stop making enemies
And let's face the facts,
People will always need people,
Yes
People will always need people.

CHILDREN OF THE SEWERS

Nobody knows how many children
Live in stinking sewers,
The experts have lost count of how many
Children, beg, steal and die
In the stinking sewers.
Some people don't even call
Children who live in the sewers children,
They call them vermin and filth,
Tramps and thieves.
Unable to understand what it's like to live
In nooks and crannies,
They step over, walk over, walk around
Bypass and ignore these children,
Who could be their children
Before they know it.
Unwilling to lend a hand
They make themselves busy,
Too busy to lend a hand,
They wrap themselves in big houses
Big cars, big money, big swimming pools,
And they have big fences
To stop them seeing
The small children
Who live in the stinking sewers.

Ask the children of the sewers
Why they live in the sewers
And you will hear horror stories,
Stories of loveless lives,
Stories of rejection,
Stories of abuse,
These children's only fault
Was having the wrong parents.

So if there are children living in the sewers
In your city,
Or if you see the children of the sewers
On television,
Before you walk by or
Change channels,
Just think of how lucky you are,
Think of where your waste is going
Think of what you do with what you don't want,
And remember that sewers
Were not made for children,
But then again nor were violent homes,
Families that don't care
Or people that don't respect children.
You don't need the World Health Organization
To tell you that a sewer is one of
The most unsafe places in a city,
But for some children
A stinking unsafe sewer
Is the safest place they know.

SIGHTS AND SOUNDS

There are
More than
Six thousand
Different
Languages
Spoken
On Earth.

There is
No person
On Earth
Who can speak
Them all.

Every person
On Earth
Could learn
To speak
Any language
On Earth.

There are
Some languages
That are not
Spoken.

Languages
Like people
Have family trees.

Languages
Like people
Are all precious.

Languages
Like people
Can disappear.

Languages are
Like people

Respect your tongue.

Sign languages
Are
Crucial

Protect your hands.

ONE FOUR ALL

There are
More than
Six billion
Individual
People
On Earth.

There is
No one person
Who knows
Every person
On Earth.

Every person
On Earth
Could spend
Their whole life
Learning
About themselves.

Some people
Spend their lives
Teaching people
To be people.

People
Like languages
Have family trees.

People
All over
Are all gorgeous.

People
Like languages
Can disappear.

People are
Like you

Respect people.

All people
Are
Vital

Protect people.

EVERY BODY IS DOING IT

In Hawaii they Hula
They Tango in Argentina
They Reggae in Jamaica
And they Rumba down in Cuba,
In Trinidad and Tobago
They do the Calypso
And in Spain the Spanish
They really do Flamenco.

In the Punjab they Bhangra
How they dance Kathak in India
Over in Guatemala
They dance the sweet Marimba,
Even foxes dance a lot
They invented the Fox Trot,
In Australia it's true
They dance to the Didgeridoo.

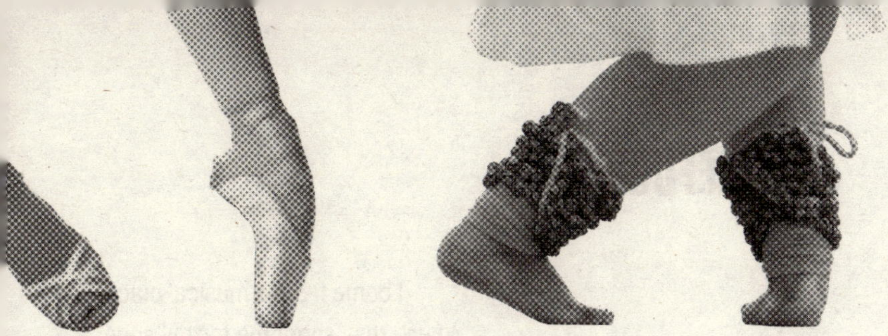

In Kenya they Benga
They Highlife in Ghana
They dance Ballet all over
And Rai dance in Algeria,
They Jali in Mali
In Brazil they Samba
And the girls do Belly Dancing
In the northern parts of Africa.

Everybody does the Disco
From Baghdad to San Francisco
Many folk with razzamataz
Cannot help dancing to Jazz,
They do the Jig in Ireland
And it is really true
They still Morris dance in England
When they can find time to.

WE REFUGEES

I come from a musical place
Where they shoot me for my song
And my brother has been tortured
By my brother in my land.

I come from a beautiful place
Where they hate my shade of skin
They don't like the way I pray
And they ban free poetry.

I come from a beautiful place
Where girls cannot go to school
There you are told what to believe
And even young boys must grow beards.

I come from a great old forest
I think it is now a field
And the people I once knew
Are not there now.

We can all be refugees
Nobody is safe,
All it takes is a mad leader
Or no rain to bring forth food,
We can all be refugees
We can all be told to go,
We can be hated by someone
For being someone.

I come from a beautiful place
Where the valley floods each year
And each year the hurricane tells us
That we must keep moving on.

I come from an ancient place
All my family were born there
And I would like to go there
But I really want to live.

I come from a sunny, sandy place
Where tourists go to darken skin
And dealers like to sell guns there
I just can't tell you what's the price.

I am told I have no country now
I am told I am a lie
I am told that modern history books
May forget my name.

We can all be refugees
Sometimes it only takes a day,
Sometimes it only takes a handshake
Or a paper that is signed.
We all came from refugees
Nobody simply just appeared,
Nobody's here without a struggle,
And why should we live in fear
Of the weather or the troubles?
We all came here from somewhere.

I LUV ME MUDDER

I luv me mudder an me mudder luvs me
We cum so far from over de sea,
We heard dat de streets were paved wid gold
Sometimes it's hot, sometimes it's cold,
I luv me mudder an me mudder luvs me
We try fe live in harmony
Yu might know her as Valerie
But to me she's just my mummy.

She shouts at me daddy so loud sometime
She's always been a friend of mine
She's always doing de best she can
She works so hard down ina Englan,
She's always singin sum kinda song
She has big muscles an she very, very strong,
She likes pussycats an she luvs cashew nuts
An she don't bother wid no if an buts.

I luv me mudder an me mudder luvs me
We come so far from over de sea,
We heard dat de streets were paved wid gold
Sometimes it's hot, sometimes it's cold,
I luv her and whatever we do
Dis is a luv I know is true,
My people, I'm talking to yu
Me an my mudder we luv yu too.

BRIGHT AND BEAUTIFUL

Sun shines
Stars shine
Moon shines.
Trees shine
Life shines
Good shines.
Day shines
Night shines
Earth shines
White shines
Black shines
You shine.

CONFESSIONS OF A RUNNER

On my first day at school
My sister cried and cried
On my first day at school
I could have died and died
On my first day at school
My twin embarrassed me
On my first day at school
I learnt schoolology.

On my second day at school
My sister wouldn't come
On my second day at school
She was dragged there by my Mom
On my second day at school
I came dressed in pink
On my second day at school
I was made to think.

On my third day at school
I explored everywhere
On my third day at school
I fell offa my chair
On my third day at school
We all went for a swim
On my third day at school
I cried just like my twin.

On my fourth day at school
They made me run in shorts
On my fourth day at school
I discovered sports
On my fourth day at school
I ran fast and far
On my fourth day at school
I earned myself a star.

On my fifth day at school
We had tomato crumble
On my fifth day at school
I began to grumble
On my fifth day at school
My teacher got stuck in red tape
On my fifth day at school
Me and my twin escaped.

THERE'S SOMEONE

It may not be the one you're with
They may not have much love to give,
It may not be the girl next door
Or that nice boy on the first floor,
It may not be the friend you taught
Who helps you out when you're distraught,
You may not know this one that well
But there's someone who loves you.

It may not be the one you kissed
It may not be the one you've missed,
You may think someone is your friend
But then you find that they pretend,
When you are down and you are out
When you're in tears, sad, and in doubt,
Life may feel like a living hell
But there's someone who loves you.

JAMAICAN SUMMERS

Jamaican summers are so hot,
But all over Jamaica
People walk around saying
Dis is cool
Dat is cool
She is cool
Or he's so cool.

Jamaican summers are so hot,
Dat all over Jamaica
Parents are always saying
Drink yu coconut water
Drink yu kisko pops
Drink yu mountain water
Yu muss drink a lot.

Jamaican summers are so hot,
Dat all over Jamaica
People chill out in de shade
Sleep under trees
Or travel fe miles
To find cool breeze.

In Jamaica,
Very soon after summer
Comes de winter,
But beware
Let me give yu a warning me friend,
Jamaican winters are **so hot.**

WE PEOPLE TOO

I have dreams of summer days
Of running freely on the lawn
I luv a lazy Sunday morn
Like many others do.
I luv my family always
I luv clear water in a stream
Oh yes I cry and yes I dream
We dogs are people too.

When I have time I luv sightseeing
You may not want to see my face
But you and me must share a space
Like many others do.
Please think of me, dear human being,
It seems that I'm always in need
I have a family to feed
We mice are people too.

They say we're really dangerous
But we too like to feel and touch
And we like music very much
Like many others do.
Most of us are not poisonous
I have a little lovely face
I move around with style and grace
We snakes are people too.

And I, dear folk, am small and great
My friends call me the mighty Bruce
I luv to drink pure orange juice
Like many others do.
I hope you all appreciate
We give you all a helping hand
When me and my friends turn the land
We worms are people too.

I don't mind if you stand and stare
But know that I have luv no end
And my young ones I will defend
Like many others do.
When you see me in the air
Remember that I know the worth
Of all us who share the earth
We birds are people too.

I need fresh air and exercise
I need to safely cross the road,
I carry such a heavy load
Like many others do.
Don't only judge me by my size
Ask any veterinarian
I'm just a vegetarian
We cows are people too.

Water runs straight off my smooth back
And I hold my head high with pride
I like my children at my side
Like many others do.
I don't care if you're white or black
If you like land or air or sea
I want to see more unity
We ducks are people too.

I think living is so cool
And what I really like the most
Is kiss chase and I luv brown toast
Like many others do.
I hang around in a big school
I only need a little sleep
I like thinking really deep
We fish are people too.

I luv the cows I love the trees
And I would rather you not smoke
For if you smoke then I would choke
Like many others do.
I beg you do not squash me please
I do not want to cause you harm
I simply want you to stay calm
We flies are people too.

My name is Thomas Tippy Tops
Billy is not my name
I've learnt to live with fame
Like many others do.
I once was on Top of the Pops
On TV I sang loud
My parents were so proud
We goats are people too.

I luv to walk among the fern
I'm thankful for each night and day
I really luv to holiday
Like many others do.
I've read the books and my concern
Is why do we always look bad?
My friends don't think I'm raving mad
We wolves are people too.

A lovely garden makes me smile
A good joke makes me croak
One day I want to own a boat
Like many others do
I'd luv to see the river Nile
I'd luv my own sandcastle
I really want to travel
We frogs are people too.

Please do not call me horrid names
Think of me as a brother
I'm quite nice you'll discover
Like many others do.
If you're my friend then call me James
I'll be your friend for ever more
I'll be the one that you adore
We pigs are people too.

We really need this planet
And we want you to be aware
We just don't have one spare
Not any of us do.

We dogs, we goats
We mice, we snakes
Even we worms
Are really great,
We birds, we cows
We ducks, we frogs
Are just trying to do our jobs
We wolves, we fish
We pigs, we flies
Could really open up your eyes
And all we want to say to you
Is that
We all are people too.

BE COOL MANKIND

My love for you
Is oh so true,
Be good mankind, be good mankind,
And let us be as one people,
Be good mankind, be good.

Let's live some more
Abandon war,
Be safe mankind, be safe mankind,
And let us live our dreams people,
Be safe mankind, be safe.

There is one race
The living race,
Spread love mankind, spread love mankind,
And let's be peace and love people
Spread love mankind, spread love.

Don't get me wrong
My love is strong,
Be cool mankind, be cool mankind,
And let us live as one people,
Be cool mankind, be cool.

Index of First Lines

THOUGHTS?

IDEAS?

POEMS?

Benjamin Zephaniah was born in Handsworth, Birmingham in 1958, a place he proudly hailed as 'the Jamaican capital of Europe'.

He grew up listening to tapes of Jamaican dub poetry, which combined reggae rhythms with lyrics that highlighted political and social issues. He began performing poetry aged ten and quickly gained a reputation in his area.

After moving to London, his reputation continued to grow and in 1980 he published *Pen Rhythm*, his first book of poetry. He became known for his electrifying performances, and his poetry was often heard at political demonstrations and youth gatherings. Radical, relevant and exciting, Benjamin's poetry confronted racial tension, police brutality and unemployment.

In 1994, he published *Talking Turkeys*, his first poetry book for children. By the late 1990s, Benjamin was appearing regularly on radio and TV, championing poetry, culture and equality. He famously rejected an appointment as Officer of the Order of the British Empire (OBE) in 2003, as it was inconsistent with his anti-colonial beliefs. He also supported many charitable organizations and was awarded more than sixteen honorary doctorates for his contributions to literature, education and the arts.

Benjamin passed away on 7 December 2023, at the age of sixty-five.